ARLENE FELTMAN SAILHAC'S
DE GUSTIBUS GREAT COOKS' COOKBOOKS

Low-Fat Cooking

ARLENE FELTMAN SAILHAC'S
DE GUSTIBUS GREAT COOKS' COOKBOOKS

Low-Fat Cooking

PHOTOGRAPHS BY TOM ECKERLE

DESIGN BY MARTIN LUBIN

BLACK DOG & LEVENTHAL

NEW YORK

Published by

Black Dog & Leventhal
151 West 19th Street
New York, NY 10011

Distributed by

Workman Publishing Company
708 Broadway
New York, NY 10003

Manufactured in Hong kong

ISBN: 1-884822-34-7

h g f e d c b a

Eggplant and Crab Garbure with Cumin and Tomato Confit; Broiled Pompano with Pickles and Vegetables from *Cooking with Daniel Boulud* by Daniel Boulud. Copyright © 1993 Daniel Boulud. Reprinted by permission of Random House, Inc., New York.

Big Easy Seafood-Okra Gumbo from *Emeril's New Orleans Cooking* by Emeril Lagasse and Jessie Tirsch. Copyright © 1993 Emeril Lagasse. Reprinted by permission of William Morrow and Company, Inc., New York.

Sweet Pepper and Yellow Pepper Soup from *The New Basics Cookbook* by Julie Russo and Sheila Lukins. Copyright © 1989 Julie Russo and Sheila Lukins. Reprinted by permission of Workman Publishing, New York.

Jamaican Jerk Chicken with Banana-Guava Ketchup from *The Thrill of the Grill: Techniques, Recipes & Down-Home Barbecue* by Chris Schlesinger and John Willoughby. Copyright © 1990 Chris Schlesinger and John Willoughby. Reprinted by permission of William Morrow and Company, Inc., New York.

London Broil "Smoke Gets in Your House" Style with Lime-Marinated Red Onions and Chunky Pineapple Catsup; Parlsey Salad with Bulgur, Mint, and Tomatoes; and Grilled Peaches with Blue Cheese and Sweet Balsamic Glaze adapted from *Big Flavors of the Hot Sun: Hot Recipes and Cool Tips from the Spice Zone* by Chris Schlesinger and John Willoughby. Copyright © 1994 Chris Schlesinger and John Willoughby. Reprinted by permission of William Morrow and Company, Inc., New York.

DEDICATION

I dedicate this book to my family, which loves to eat:

My parents, Adelaide and Stanley Kessler

My sister, brother-in-law, and niece, Gayle, Stanley, and Amy Miller

My Grandma Berdie, who opened my eyes to food

And to Alain Sailhac and Todd Feltman, the two "men in my life who are my favorite dining partners."

ACKNOWLEDGMENTS

During the fifteen-year existence of De Gustibus at Macy's, many people have given their support and encouragment.

First, my profound thanks to all the wonderful chefs and cooks who have taught at De Gustibus at Macy's. A special thanks to: Paul Bartolotta, Mario Batali, Jean-Michel Bergougnoux, Daniel Boulud, Jane Brody, Ed Brown, Patrick Clark, Gordon Hamersley, Ron Hook, Patricia Jamieson, Emeril Lagasse, Sheila Lukins, Mark Militello, Georges Perrier, Douglas Rodriguez, Chris Schlesinger, Sally Schneider, Nancy Silverton, Mark Peel, and Marie Simmons.

Thanks to my priceless assistants who are always there for me in a million ways: Jane Asche, Barbara Bjorn, Pam Carey, Corinne Gherardi, Yonina Jacobs, Nancy Robbins, and Betti Zucker.

Thanks to Barbara Teplitz for all her help and support throughout the years, and to Gertrud Yampierre for holding the office together.

Thanks to Ruth Schwartz for believing in the concept of De Gustibus and helping to orchestrate its initiation at Macy's.

Thanks to everyone at Macy's Herald Square who have supported De Gustibus at Macy's since its inception, with special notice to the Public Relations and Advertising Departments who helped spread the word.

Thanks to J.P. Leventhal and Pamela Horn of Black Dog & Leventhal Publishers for providing the vehicle to put our cooking classes into book form and for being so encouraging.

A special thanks to Jane Asche for her help in the beginning stages of the book.

Thanks to Tom Eckerle for his magical photographs; Ceci Gallini for her impeccable taste and prop design; and Roscoe Betsill, whose food styling really took this project to another level.

Thanks for supplying the exquisite props for the photographs to Takashimaya, New York City.

Thanks to Marty Lubin for his wonderful design.

Thanks to Mary Goodbody and Judith Sutton for making the book "user friendly."

Thanks to my agent Judith Weber for her help and advice.

Special thanks to Judith Choate, who shaped all my words into meaningful prose and never ceased to amaze me with her knowledge of food and her patience and calm, and to Steve Pool for getting these words into the computer with smiles and enthusiasm.

Heartfelt thanks to the entire Kobrand Corporation, purveyors of fine wine, especially Cathleen Burke and Kimberly Charles for opening the door for the marriage of fine wine and great food for the last ten years.

Finally, thanks to all the faithful De Gustibus customers who have made all our classes spring to life.

Contents

FOREWORD   6

INTRODUCTION   7

THE COOKS   8

TECHNIQUES   12

A WORD ABOUT THE NUTRITIONAL ANALYSES   13

PANTRY RECIPES   14

Appetizers and Soups   16

Salads and Side Dishes   34

Entrées   43

    POULTRY   45

    MEAT   51

    FISH AND SEAFOOD   60

    PASTA   69

Desserts   75

SUGGESTED MENUS   88

GLOSSARY   89

INDEX   92

Foreword

Fifteen years ago, the popularity of cooking classes was growing all over the United States. While interest was high, New Yorkers could not always fit an ongoing series of classes into their busy schedules. Demonstration classes seemed to me to be the answer, and De Gustibus was born. What began as four chefs and an electric frying pan on a stage developed into more than 350 chefs and cooking teachers demonstrating their specialties in a professionally equipped kitchen for groups of fervent food-lovers.

When we started De Gustibus in 1980, we had no inkling of the variety of new cuisines that would become an integral part of American cooking. Since then, we have discovered New World Cuisine, Florida Cuisine, Light Cooking, Fusion Cooking, Cajun Cooking, Southwest Cooking —you name it! As American and international cuisines have changed and our tastes have broadened, De Gustibus has stayed on the cutting edge of the culinary experience. We have invited teachers, cooks, and chefs to De Gustibus both because of their level of recognition in the food world and because of their challenging, unique, current, and, above all, noteworthy cooking styles.

The goal of the cooking demonstrations at De Gustibus is to make the art of the grand master chefs and cooks accessible for the home kitchen. Each chef leads the way and holds out a helping hand to the home cook. The results depend as much on the cook's wit, self-confidence, and interest as they do on a great recipe. Thus, students, and now readers of this book, can learn to master the recipes of the most sophisticated chefs and cooks.

The reason De Gustibus demonstration classes are so popular is that they allow the novice the opportunity to feel the passion—as well as to see each professional chef's or cook's technique, order, and discipline. By observing how each chef's personality influences the final product, serious home cooks gain the confidence to trust their own tastes and instincts. New and unfamiliar ingredients, untried techniques, and even a little dazzle all find a place in the amateur's kitchen.

We have changed the format of this book from the menus we provided in the first five books in the series to individual recipes organized into traditional categories: appetizers, soups, salads and side dishes, entrées, and desserts. We did this because we wanted to present only those dishes with a judicious use of fat that had been featured at De Gustibus, which translate into some of the best and most popular light, healthful dishes demonstrated throughout the years. Each dish is designed to serve six people, unless otherwise noted. All were prepared in class, and I have altered them only slightly to accommodate our requirements for light, relatively low-fat dishes. Each has been tested and streamlined for the home kitchen. If you have not tried this kind of cooking—fearing you will lose flavor and pleasure at the expense of "health"—these recipes are a simple way to introduce this style of cooking into your repertoire in all their delicious glory.

THE *MISE EN PLACE*

The organizational technique known as the *mise en place* is the most valuable lesson we at De Gustibus have learned from the pros. (Translated from the French, *mise en place* literally means "putting in place.") We strongly urge you to cook this way: Place all ingredients for a particular recipe on, or in, individual trays, plates, or bowls, according to the specific steps in the recipes. Each item should be washed, chopped, measured, separated—whatever is called for— before you begin to cook. Taking the time to organize the ingredients will insure greater success with every recipe.

Mise en place tray

Introduction

Health-conscious, low-fat, and low-calorie cooking did not play much of a role in the early development of De Gustibus. In our beginning years, even if we did have dietary concerns, we were content to let the chefs prepare the foods they liked and then we would try to adapt them to our own requirements.

Then, about ten years ago, I began to notice more people, both chefs and students, rethinking their way of eating. As the American fitness craze exploded, the dream vacation became a visit to a spa rather than the gastronomic "tour de France" of years past. Almost as quickly, I became aware that neither extreme was satisfying. Spa devotees became sneak eaters and *foie gras* fanatics always felt guilty.

During this period, chefs from many of the world's great spas were presented at De Gustibus. They introduced us to an entirely new way of eating, but many of the recipes that they featured substituted low-calorie ingredients for the "real" thing and we found the deception unfulfilling. Consequently, our low-calorie classes were never integrated into our chef's programs, as health-conscious eating seemed an anathema to fine dining.

As the years passed, more and more elements of health awareness entered the kitchen at De Gustibus. Many more cookbooks on healthy cuisines, as well as entire magazines devoted to "lighter" cooking, were being published. Students became increasingly conscious of the kinds of foods that were on menus both at home and in restaurants. Chefs from all over the world were rethinking their traditional methods of cooking as well as their own way of eating.

The world leader in the evolution of the integration of health-conscious eating into fine dining was France's Michel Guerard. His *cuisine minceur*, based on classic French *haute cuisine*, was much less elaborate and much more calorie-conscious than the *nouvelle cuisine* that almost all chefs had experimented with in the early seventies. With this French groundwork making health-conscious dining more acceptable, the De Gustibus classroom welcomed many chefs and cooking teachers producing heart- and mind-healthy dishes that were beautifully flavored, incredibly well seasoned, and filled with a balance of ingredients and textures.

Food writers and cooks such as Marie Simmons, Jane Brody, Sally Schneider, and Patsy Jamieson gave us delicious low-fat recipes that were perfect for our day-to-day meals. Great chefs presented dishes that were intensely flavored with herbs and spices and prepared using methods that cut much of the use of fats and creams. All cuisines were represented in these alternative preparations—and what delicious meals we have had.

For this book, I have taken many recipes just as they were presented at De Gustibus. However, some recipes, particularly those from chefs not generally known for health-conscious cooking, have been revised (with the chef's approval and assistance) to conform to our lighter, more healthful requirements. While the nutritional analysis preceding each recipe lists the percentage of fat from calories, it behooves you to note the total calories and fat grams as well. At times the percentage of fat may be relatively high, but the overall calories and fat grams are quite low. Because I make no claims that this is a "diet" book or a stringent low-fat treatise, I have worked to keep the percentage of calories from fat below forty percent (and often much lower)—although I know many other low-fat books insist on a lower percentage. I hope my readers will accept these recipes in the spirit in which they are offered: reasonably light, healthful dishes prepared by master chefs, meant to eaten in moderation as part of an overall fresh, low-fat, day-to-day diet. Additionally, I do, from time to time, give alternative choices for optional sauces and garnishes to further reduce calories and fat. A section of suggested menus will also help you balance your meals. This gives you, the home cook, the option to choose the version that sits most comfortably on your table.

It now appears that healthful cooking is not an isolated, soon-to-disappear addition to the restaurant and home kitchen. Chefs are continuing to look for safer, saner ways of preparing satisfying meals, and home cooks are eager to learn healthier methods of cooking. Great ingredients, well seasoned, easily prepared, and served in sensible portions are coming together to make meals that make us feel as good about ourselves as we feel when we are eating them.

The Cooks

Paul Bartolotta: Paul first came to De Gustibus when he was chef de cuisine at San Domenico Restaurant in New York City. He was not so much cook as translator for his mentor, Valentino Mercatelli, of the famed San Domenico Ristorante in Italy. He subsequently achieved great success cooking his own contemporary interpretation of classic Italian dishes at Spiaggia in Chicago. His Bow Tie Pasta with Mussels and Zucchini is a pristine example of Paul Bartolotta's light touch.

Mario Batali: With the recent opening of his personal trattoria-style restaurant, Pó, Mario is a most welcome newcomer to New York's Italian restaurant scene. Mario's cooking is rustic, simply prepared, but full of memorable flavor. His contributions of Asparagus and Morel Bruschetta, Fusilli with Twenty-Minute Tomato Sauce, Hot Chiles, and Arugula, and a cool Lamb Salad with Flageolets, Cumin, and Roasted Peppers reflect his relaxed, full-flavored style.

Jean-Michel Bergougnoux: Jean-Michel is one of the great proponents of modern French cuisine. He first came to DeGustibus when he was at Le Régence at The Plaza Athenée in New York. His superb technique took him on to Lutèce and Le Cygne, two of New York's premier French restaurants. Diners are now being dazzled at L'Absinthe, Jean-Michel's much-heralded addition to New York's French restaurant scene. Braised Beef with Bean, Zucchini, and Pepper Salad is a fine example of his flavorful cooking style.

Daniel Boulud: Not only is Daniel Boulud skilled at the preparation of *haute* gastronomy, he can and does create low-fat, low-calorie menus at the drop of a patron's hat. I first met a very young Daniel many meals ago during his early years in New York. He has gone on to receive the highest accolades from all over the world for his cooking at Le Cirque and, more recently, at his own 4-star Restaurant Daniel in New York City, as well as for his cookbook, *Cooking with Daniel Boulud*. This brilliant, still-young chef has garnered awards for the best restaurant in the United States from Gault-Millau and the *International Herald Tribune*, and has also been named Chef of the Year by the James Beard Foundation. In our low-fat quests Daniel has given us Eggplant and Crab Garbure with Cumin and Tomato Confit, Broiled Pompano with Pickles and Vegetables, and a most delicious Banana-Pineapple Shake.

Jane Brody: Jane is the Personal Health columnist for *The New York Times* and she certainly takes her job seriously. She not only eats well all the time, she exercises with commitment and vigor. Once she came to teach right after ice skating, looking the perfect picture of endorsement for her chosen field. Jane has written seven books highlighting a healthy lifestyle, ranging from *Secrets of Good Health* to her series of *Jane Brody's Good Food* books. Jane has shared three fabulous low-fat recipes with us: a Mediterranean-inspired chickpea appetizer, a savory green bean salad, and an enticing Carrot-Raisin Cake.

Ed Brown: Ed came to De Gustibus on the praises of many of our regulars, who kept telling me about his innovative way with seafood at Tropica, a trend-setting New York City restaurant. His interest in working with impeccably fresh, unusual seafood has made him quite a piscine authority. He confessed to us that he had been so inspired by what he had learned working in the classroom with home cooks that he wrote *Modern Seafood Cooking* just for us. Ed is now chef at the SeaGrill, in Rockefeller Center, and the two fish dishes we feature show the range of his style. Grilled Swordfish and Fennel with Charred Tomatoes, Oil-Roasted Garlic, and Thirty-Year-Old Balsamic Vinegar is filled with Italian flavors, while the Striped Bass with Mango-Black Bean Salsa, Chayote Squash, and Mango Sauce would be at home in the Caribbean.

Patrick Clark: Not only does Patrick Clark create food that is deliciously well seasoned and interesting, he always brings us recipes that are accessible to the home cook. He first came to De Gustibus when he was Executive Chef for cafes Odeon and Luxembourg in New York City. He again taught while he was chef/owner of Metro. He was a New York treasure. He then abandoned us for California and subsequently Washington, DC, but in 1995 our luck changed, and Patrick returned to New York as chef at the wildly successful Tavern on the Green. Voted Best Chef in the Mid-Atlantic by the James Beard Foundation in 1994, Patrick was also one of the original thirteen chefs chosen by Julia Child for her master chef series. The low-fat, Mediterranean-inspired Roasted Salmon with Moroccan Barbecue Sauce served with Couscous and Sautéed Savoy Cabbage is Patrick Clark at his best.

Gordon Hamersley: I actually knew of Gordon Hamersley before his Boston restaurant, Hamersley's Bistro, came to exist. In 1987, I met his wife, who told me that she was leaving her job to help her husband open a restaurant. They went on to become a very important part of Boston's burgeoning restaurant action and Gordon came to teach at De Gustibus. His wonderful manner and use of familiar ingredients combined in unexpected ways have made him a classroom favorite. The two dishes we present are excellent examples of Gordon's quick but gutsy approach: Braised Wild Mushrooms with Roasted Garlic Toasts and Asparagus Salad with Littleneck Clams and Thyme.

Ron Hook: Ron Hook was brought to my attention by Patricia Bell of *Gourmet* magazine, who had experienced his cooking while doing a story on the Doral Saturnia International Spa Resort in Miami, Florida. She described his food as "real" yet low in fat and calories, with delicious savor. When he taught at De Gustibus, Ron was able to share his food philosophy, which is based on the nutritional value of what we eat, as well as how to balance the different food groups to make meals with great symmetry. Ron is now bringing his skills at healthy cooking to the spa guests at the Canyon Ranch in the Berkshire hills of Massachusetts. We are delighted that his proximity to New York City now makes him more accessible to the De Gustibus classroom.

Patricia Jamieson: Patsy Jamieson is one of the very few teachers at De Gustibus who specializes in low-fat cooking. As kitchen director for Telemedia Communications USA, she oversees all of the recipe development and testing programs for *Eating Well, the Magazine of Food & Health* as well as for *Eating Well* books. Her trim body and energetic personality are a tribute to the doctrines she espouses and serve to encourage all of us to practice what she teaches. Co-editor of *The Eating Well Cookbook, The Eating Well Recipe Rescue Cookbooks,* and *The Eating Well Rush Hour Cookbook,* Patsy offers us Caramelized Onion Pizza, Roasted Turkey Breast with Port and Dried Cranberry Sauce, Roasted Sweet Potatoes, Ziti with Lentils and Kale, Wild Rice-Orzo Pilaf and Blackberry-Rhubarb Tart.

Emeril Lagasse: Emeril's first De Gustibus class was with the celebrated Ella Brennan, his then boss at Commander's Palace in New Orleans. They had just collaborated on *The Commander's Palace Cookbook* and Emeril, as executive chef, absolutely dazzled the class with his exuberant style and his vivid description of "New Creole" food. On his subsequent visits, Emeril was first the proud owner of the award-winning Emeril's, then of another restaurant, Nola, and then author of *Emeril's New New Orleans Cooking.* Although most of Emeril's cooking falls far away from the low-fat category, his Big Easy Seafood-Okra Gumbo gives a taste of the old style without the traditional fats and roux.

Sheila Lukins: Sheila Lukins always teaches to a sold-out class. Not only is everything she prepares delicious, she makes the art of entertaining accessible and fun. Plus, you just know that she has actually cooked these dishes for family and friends and relished every moment of it. Co-founder of The Silver Palate shop and products, co-author of *The Silver Palate Cookbook, The Silver Palate Good Times Cookbook,* and *The New Basics Cookbook,* author of *Sheila Lukins All Around the World Cookbook,* and food editor of *Parade* magazine, Sheila presents for this book two knockout soups that, together, make one eye-catching presentation.

Mark Militello: I first met Mark after a great meal at Mark's in North Miami Beach, Florida, where he was the executive chef. He went on to buy the spot, rename it Mark's Place, and develop his own innovative cuisine featuring ingredients indigenous to Florida. He has gone on to be named Best Chef in the region by the James Beard Foundation and one of the Best Chefs in America by *Food & Wine* magazine and to win accolades from many leading publications, as well as to open another restaurant, Mark's Los Olas, in Fort Lauderdale. Mark's love of tropical ingredients has helped him create a style of cooking that is uniquely his own. His Chilled Summer Vegetable Soup with Spanish Vinegar and Quinoa Salad will give you just a hint of his polish.

Georges Perrier: Georges is the first superstar chef I met—can it be more than twenty-five years ago? I had just moved to Philadelphia and found myself neighbors with another recent transplant, who was the chef at the acclaimed Le Panetière restaurant. He had taken Philadelphia diners by storm! Georges went on to open Le Bec-Fin, which has been considered, from the moment it opened, Philadelphia's premier dining spot. Over the years, our lives have continued to cross, so his visits to De Gustibus are rather like having an old friend come to call. The sole recipe we feature is from a class for which he was asked to create low-fat French-inspired food.

Douglas Rodriguez: Doug's star quality and wild personality burst on the scene at Yuca Restaurant in Coral Gables, Florida. Cooking what he called *Nuevo Latino* cuisine, he was garnering attention from all over the world. Always innovative and expressive, Doug now cooks at his own restaurant, Patria, in New York City, where the tropical ingredients he knows so well are setting New York foodies on their *cabezas*! Now, we can all cook with Doug through his first cookbook, *Nuevo Latino*.

Chris Schlesinger: Chris's love of spicy cuisines—both those from tropical climates and those highly seasoned—make his classes hot on the De Gustibus schedule. Additionally, his abilities at the grill appeal to even the weekend backyard cook and his classes are always standing room only. Co-owner of the East Coast Bar and Grill, Jake and Earl's, and The Blue Room and co-author of three cookbooks, *The Thrill of the Grill; Salsas, Sambals, Chutneys, and Chow Chow;* and *Big Flavors of the Hot Sun*, Chris is always welcome at De Gustibus.

Sally Schneider: Sally Schneider is absolutely passionate about teaching low-calorie cooking. She is so good at turning good-for-you food into good-to-eat food that she is one of the De Gustibus classroom favorites. In 1991, Sally won the James Beard Foundation Cookbook Award for *The Art of Low-Calorie Cooking*, and in 1995 she won the foundation's Journalism Award for her *Saveur* article "Truffles, White and Black." Sally has certainly introduced thousands to *The New Way to Cook*, the title of her forthcoming cookbook.

Nancy Silverton and **Mark Peel:** This is a spectacular duo—Nancy with her award-winning desserts and Mark with his powerhouse cooking. What a show they gave the De Gustibus classroom. We even had an extra bit of drama when Mark did his lamb flambé—I thought our Mylar mirrors were going to ignite. But Mark knew what he was doing and, even more importantly, knew how to give explicit directions for the home cook to duplicate his

extravaganza of fantastically flavored lamb. They are co-owners of Campanile restaurant and La Brea Bakery in Los Angeles, and co-authors of *Mark Peel and Nancy Silverton at Home—Two Chefs Cook for Family and Friends*. Nancy alone gave us her marvelous book, *Desserts*. They make you feel that they love entertaining their friends and teaching novice cooks as much as they love to cook.

Marie Simmons: Marie Simmons is one of the most exuberant teachers ever to appear at De Gustibus. She is a great proponent of food that is quick to prepare, uses lots of fresh ingredients, and is filled with big flavors. The result: light meals, perfect for the weeknight cook. Author of many books, including *The Light Touch, Italian Light Cooking,* and *Rice, the Amazing Grain,* Marie often worked with the late Richard Sax, with whom she wrote *Lighter, Quicker, Better*. Marie says that "the heart of my cooking is the fact that I really love to feed people, and that's why I love to teach at De Gustibus—there are always so many hungry people to feed!"

Techniques

CUTTING VEGETABLES

Into julienne: Using a small, very sharp knife, a mandoline, or an inexpensive vegetable slicer, cut vegetables into thin, uniform sticks, usually about $1/4$ inch thick and 1 to 2 inches long. This process is easiest when each vegetable is first cut into uniform pieces. For example, trim a bell pepper into two or three evenly shaped pieces and then cut into julienne.

Into dice: Trim vegetables into uniform rectangles. Using a very sharp knife, cut into strips ranging in width from $1/8$ to $1/4$ inch, depending upon the size dice you require. Lay the strips together and cut into even dice by crosscutting into squares $1/8$ to $1/4$ inch across. When dicing bell peppers, it is particularly important to trim all membrane and ridges so that you have an absolutely smooth rectangle.

BLANCHING VEGETABLES

Place trimmed vegetables (or fruit) into rapidly boiling water for a brief period, often no more than 30 seconds, then immediately drain and plunge into ice cold water to stop the cooking process. Blanching serves to set color and flavor, firm up the flesh, and/or loosen the skin.

ROASTING PEPPERS AND CHILES

Using a fork with a heat-proof handle, hold the pepper or chile over a gas burner as close to the flame as possible, without actually placing in the flame, until the skin puffs and is charred black. Turn as necessary to ensure that the entire pepper or chile is charred. Place the charred pepper or chile in a plastic bag, seal, and allow to steam for about 10 minutes.

Remove the pepper or chile from bag and pull off the charred skin. Stem and seed. Dice, chop, or purée as required.

If using an electric stove, place the pepper or chile in a large dry cast-iron skillet over medium-high heat. Cook slowly, turning frequently, until completely charred. Proceed as above.

To roast several peppers or chiles at a time, place them on a sheet pan under a preheated broiler. Position as close to the heat as possible without touching the flame or coil and roast until the skin puffs and is charred black. Turn to char the entire peppers or chiles as necessary. Proceed as described above.

When roasting chiles, remember that their oils are very potent. As the skin blackens, you may feel burning in your eyes and throat, which may cause some momentary discomfort. It is advisable to roast a large number of chiles under a broiler, rather than on top of the stove, to contain the potency.

ROASTING VEGETABLES

Preheat the oven to 350 degrees F.

For root vegetables, trim and peel if desired. If small, cut in half lengthwise; if large, cut into quarters. Toss with a small amount of olive oil and salt and pepper to taste. For tomatoes, cut in half, and seed if desired. For onions, peel if desired. If large, cut in half. Rub with olive oil, salt, and pepper.

Place the vegetables on a heavy-duty baking sheet and bake until tender when pierced with a fork.

NOTE: To slow-roast tomatoes, cut as above, and bake at 200 degrees F for about 3 hours, or until they are almost dried. Alternatively, if you have a gas oven with a pilot light, lay cut-side down on a baking sheet and place in the oven with the pilot light on for at least 12 hours, or until almost dry.

ZESTING CITRUS FRUITS

For strips of zest or chopped zest, using a vegetable peeler, a sharp paring knife, or a zester, remove *only* the thin layer of oily colored outer skin of any citrus fruit (the white pith beneath the colored skin tastes bitter). Then cut into thinner strips or chop as required. For grated zest, carefully remove the colored outer skin using the smallest holes of a metal grater.

Preparing Chiles

The intense heat of the chile is mainly found in the seeds, the placenta (the fleshy part near the stem end), and the white veins that run down the inside of the chile. When removing these parts, some cooks prefer to use rubber gloves. Whether you choose to wear gloves or not, be sure to wash your hands well after working with chiles. Also, keep your hands away from your eyes and mouth until your hands are clean and the chile oil has completely dissipated. Both fresh and dried chiles can be stemmed, seeded, and deveined before use. Dried chiles are frequently reconstituted by soaking them in hot water or broth for about 30 minutes, or until softened.

Using an Ice Water Bath

Place the container of hot cooked food in a larger container (or a plugged sink) filled with enough ice and cold water to come at least halfway up the sides of the hot container. Stir the food from time to time to speed cooling. An ice water bath is used to cool foods quickly in order to halt cooking and prevent bacteria formation. Foods cooled in this fashion are often further chilled with refrigeration or freezing.

Using a Mortar and Pestle

The ingredients to be ground or pulverized are placed in the mortar, a bowl-shaped container. The pestle, an easily gripped hand-sized club with a rounded or pointed end, is rotated, pressing the ingredient against the bottom and sides of the mortar, until the desired consistency is reached. A mortar and pestle, one of the world's most ancient kitchen devices, may be made of hardwood, marble, or glazed stone.

Cooking Pasta

Pasta, whether fresh or dried, should be cooked in ample boiling salted water just until it is *al dente*, or tender but still firm to the bite. As a rule of thumb, 2 gallons of water is enough to cook 1 pound of pasta. To ensure the best possible taste and texture, most chefs add salt once the water comes to a boil, before adding the pasta to the pot.

A Word about the Nutritional Analyses

I have analyzed the recipes for grams of total fat and saturated fat, as well as for total calories and the percentage of fat from calories. As explained in the Introduction, my aim was to keep the percentage of fat below 40%. The percentage of fat is far lower in many recipes. However, it is always a good idea to note the fat grams and calories as well as the percentage of fat—at times, they are quite low even though the percentage of fat is relatively high.

The nutritional values apply to the recipe they accompany. They do not take into account the secondary recipes, such as those for sauces, salads, or other accompaniments that may be included with the dish. These secondary recipes are accompanied by their own nutritional analyses. The exception to this rule is when the secondary recipe is integral to the dish, in which case its nutritional analysis is included in the overall analysis. Additionally, optional ingredients are not included in the analyses. I have deliberately broken down the elements of the recipes in this way so that you can make your own decision whether to include a sauce or garnish—or to leave it out.

Pantry Recipes

CHICKEN STOCK

MAKES ABOUT 4 CUPS
PREPARATION TIME: ABOUT 40 MINUTES
COOKING TIME: ABOUT 2 HOURS AND 30 MINUTES

Homemade stock adds a depth of flavor to a dish not possible with canned broth. However, if time is a factor, use canned chicken broth, buying those brands that are labeled "low-sodium." Do not use diluted bouillon cubes; they are excessively salty.

2 quarts (8 cups) water
2 chicken carcasses, chopped into small pieces
3 onions, chopped
1 carrot, chopped
2 ribs celery, chopped
3 sprigs fresh thyme
3 sprigs fresh parsley
1 bay leaf
1 tablespoon white peppercorns

1 In a large saucepan or stockpot, combine the water and chopped carcasses. Bring to a simmer over medium heat and skim the surface of any foam.

2 Add the onions, carrots, celery, thyme, parsley, bay leaf, and peppercorns. Bring to a boil, reduce the heat, and simmer for 1½ to 2 hours, skimming fat and foam from the surface as necessary, until reduced to 4 cups.

3 Pour the stock through a fine sieve into a clean pan and press against the solids to extract as much liquid as possible. Discard the solids. Cool to tepid (this can be done by plunging the pan into a sinkful of ice), cover, and refrigerate for 6 hours, or until all the fat particles have risen to the top. Spoon off the solidified fat and discard.

4 Bring the stock to a simmer over medium-high heat and simmer for about 30 minutes. Adjust the seasonings and use as directed in recipe.

5 To store, cool to tepid, cover, and refrigerate for 2 to 3 days or freeze in 1-cup quantities (for ease of use) for up to 3 months.

FISH STOCK

MAKES ABOUT 3 CUPS
PREPARATION TIME: ABOUT 20 MINUTES
COOKING TIME: ABOUT 25 MINUTES

Making fish stock is easier and faster then making chicken stock. Substituting canned broth is tricky in recipes calling for fish stock, but if you have no time to make stock, substitute bottled clam broth or canned low-sodium chicken broth.

2 sprigs fresh parsley
2 sprigs fresh thyme
1 small bay leaf
2 pounds fish bones (from saltwater fish such as sole, John Dory, turbot, halibut, or other very fresh, nonoily fish), chopped into pieces
2 tablespoons canola or other flavorless oil
1 small onion, chopped
1 rib celery, chopped
1 cup dry white wine

1 Using kitchen twine, make a *bouquet garni* by tying the parsley, thyme, and bay leaf together. Set aside.

2 Rinse the fish bones under cold running water.

3 In a large saucepan or stockpot, heat the oil over medium heat. Add the fish bones and vegetables. Reduce the heat and lay a piece of wax paper directly on the bones and vegetables. Cook for 10 minutes, stirring once or twice to prevent browning. (Be careful not to push the paper into the pan.)

4 Remove the wax paper. Add the wine and enough water to cover the bones and vegetables by about 2 inches. Add the *bouquet garni*. Raise the heat to high and bring to a boil. Skim the surface of all foam. Reduce the heat and simmer for 20 to 25 minutes.

5 Strain the stock through an extra-fine sieve into a clean pan. Discard the solids. Use as directed in the recipe.

6 To store, cool to tepid (this can be done by plunging the pan into a sinkful of ice), cover, and refrigerate for 2 to 3 days or freeze in 1-cup quantities (for ease of use) for up to 3 weeks.

ROASTED GARLIC

PREPARATION TIME: ABOUT 10 MINUTES
COOKING TIME: ABOUT 1 HOUR (WHOLE BULBS) OR ABOUT 15 MINUTES
  (INDIVIDUAL CLOVES)

You can roast whole garlic bulbs (heads) or separate each bulb into individual cloves.

1 or more whole garlic bulbs (heads) or 1 or more cloves garlic

1 Preheat the oven to 200 degrees F.

2 Loosely wrap the garlic in aluminum foil. Place on a pie plate or other small baking sheet. Bake for about 1 hour for a whole bulb or 15 minutes for individual cloves, or until the pulp is very soft. Unwrap and allow to cool.

For whole bulbs: Cut in half crosswise. Working from the closed ends, gently push the pulp (jam) from the skin. Discard the skin.

For individual cloves: Slit the skin using the point of a sharp knife. Peel or gently push the pulp (jam) from the skin. Discard the skin.

COOKED BEANS

MAKES ABOUT 2¹/₂ CUPS COOKED BEANS
PREPARATION TIME: ABOUT 10 MINUTES
COOKING TIME: 1 TO 2 HOURS
SOAKING TIME: AT LEAST 4 HOURS

Cooking dried beans is simply a matter of reconstituting them by soaking, followed by long, slow cooking. You can double or triple the recipe. Cooked beans keep in the freezer for up to one month. Lentils and black-eyed peas do not require soaking before cooking.

1 cup dried black, white, fava, or other beans

1 Check the beans for pebbles and other debris. Rinse them in a colander. Put the beans in a large pot and add about 10 cups of water (or 10 times the amount of the beans). Cover and let soak at room temperature for at least 4 hours. Change the water 3 or 4 times during soaking. If the beans are particularly old, let them soak for 8 hours or overnight.

2 Drain the beans, rinse with cold water, and return to the pot. Add fresh cold water to cover the beans by about 2 inches. Bring to a boil over high heat, skim the foam that rises to the surface, and reduce the heat to a simmer. Cover and cook for 1 to 2 hours, until tender, adding more water to the pot as necessary. The beans are done when they are fork-tender. Drain and proceed with the specific recipe.

NOTE: To prepare the beans by the "quick-soak method," put the beans in a large pot and add enough water to cover by 3 inches. Bring to a boil and boil for 5 minutes. Remove from the heat, cover, and soak for no less than 1 hour and no longer than 2 hours. Drain and discard the soaking water. Rinse well. Proceed with the cooking instructions above.

Appetizers

Wild Mushroom Ragout with Roasted Polenta

Braised Wild Mushrooms with Roasted Garlic Toasts

Asparagus Salad with Littleneck Clams and Thyme

Asparagus and Morel Bruschetta

Smothered Escarole on Whole Wheat Crostini

Caramelized Onion Pizza

Intercontinental Chickpea Spread

Shrimp Ceviche

Soups

Chilled Curried Tomato Soup with Cilantro Cream

Sweet Pepper and Yellow Pepper Soup

Chilled Summer Vegetable Soup with Spanish Vinegar and Quinoa Salad

Eggplant and Crab Garbure with Cumin and Tomato Confit

◁◁ *(Overleaf)* DANIEL BOULUD: Eggplant and Crab Garbure with Cumin and Tomato Confit

SALLY SCHNEIDER
Wild Mushroom Ragout with Roasted Polenta

SERVES 6
PREPARATION TIME: ABOUT 20 MINUTES
COOKING TIME: ABOUT 50 MINUTES
CHILLING TIME: ABOUT 10 MINUTES

FAT PER SERVING: 3 GRAMS
SATURATED FAT: 0.3 GRAM
CALORIES PER SERVING: 225
CALORIES FROM FAT: 14%

Rich, earthy flavor masks the low calorie content of this rustic stew. Paired with Roasted Polenta, it is a sublime first course, or even a light entrée. This can also be used as a sauce for pasta, grilled meat, or poultry. If you serve it as a sauce, to keep calories low, serve no more than one and a half cups of pasta or three and a half ounces of poultry or meat per person.

3/4 ounce dried wild mushrooms (such as porcini or morels)
6 dry-packed sun-dried tomato halves
3/4 cup boiling water
1 1/2 pounds fresh wild mushrooms in any combination (shiitakes, chanterelles, cremini, pleurottes, porcini, morels, and/or oysters)
2 teaspoons olive oil
2 large onions, chopped
4 cloves garlic, minced
3/4 cup red wine
3 sprigs fresh thyme or 3/8 teaspoon dried
5 1/4 cups canned Italian plum tomatoes, seeded and chopped, juices reserved
1 teaspoon granulated sugar
1/2 teaspoon salt, or to taste
Freshly ground black pepper to taste
Roasted Polenta (recipe follows)

SALLY SCHNEIDER: Wild Mushroom Ragout with Roasted Polenta

1 Assemble *mise en place* trays for this recipe (see page 6).

2 In a small heat-proof bowl, combine the dried mushrooms, sun-dried tomatoes, and boiling water. Cover and allow to steep for at least 15 minutes.

3 Using a damp cloth, wipe the fresh mushrooms clean. Trim off any tough stems and cut large mushrooms into 1/4-inch-thick slices. Leave small (under 1 inch in diameter) mushrooms whole. Set aside.

4 In a medium-sized saucepan, combine the oil, onions, and garlic, cover, and cook over medium heat for about 3 minutes, or until the onions begin to wilt. Uncover and

sauté for about 3 minutes, or until the onions begin to brown. Remove the pan from the heat.

5 Using a slotted spoon, scoop the sun-dried tomatoes and mushrooms from the soaking liquid into a strainer. Reserve the soaking liquid. Rinse the tomatoes and mushrooms under cold running water and press against the strainer to squeeze out all the water. Coarsely chop.

6 Without disturbing the sediment on the bottom of the bowl, spoon 7 tablespoons of the soaking liquid into the onion mixture. Add the red wine and thyme and return the pan to the heat. Bring to a boil over medium-high heat and

boil for 1 minute. Stir in the fresh mushrooms. Stir in the canned tomatoes with their liquid, the chopped dried mushrooms and tomatoes, the sugar, salt, and pepper to taste. Partially cover, bring to a simmer, and cook, stirring occasionally and breaking up the tomatoes with the back of a spoon if necessary, for about 20 minutes, or until the mushrooms are tender and the ragout has thickened. Taste and season generously with more pepper.

7 Place 4 Roasted Polenta triangles in the center of each plate. Spoon the ragout over them and serve immediately.

NOTE: If the fresh mushrooms are exceedingly gritty, wash them under cool running water. Dry them thoroughly immediately after washing. The ragout can be made up to 4 days ahead. Cover and refrigerate or, for longer storage, freeze. If the ragout is too thick, thin it with a touch of red wine, bring to a boil over medium heat, and boil for 1 minute to allow the alcohol to evaporate.

Most dry-packed sun-dried tomatoes are packed as halves. If you can only find sun-dried tomatoes packed in oil, rinse them under hot running water and pat dry.

ROASTED POLENTA

SERVES 6
FAT PER SERVING: 2.8 GRAMS
SATURATED FAT: 0.4 GRAM
CALORIES PER SERVING: 148
CALORIES FROM FAT: 17%

1¹/₂ cups coarsely ground cornmeal
1 teaspoon salt, or to taste
5¹/₄ cups cold water
2 cloves garlic, sliced
1 tablespoon extra-virgin olive oil
4 sprigs fresh rosemary, leaves only
Freshly ground black pepper to taste

1 In a large heavy saucepan, combine the cornmeal, salt, and cold water and bring to a boil over high heat, stirring constantly with a wooden spoon. Lower the heat to medium-high and cook, stirring constantly to prevent scorching, for about 10 minutes, or until the polenta pulls away from the sides and bottom of the pan.

2 Scrape the polenta onto a nonstick rimmed baking sheet and, using a spatula, pat it out into a ¹/₂-inch-thick rectangle or square. Cover with plastic wrap and refrigerate for about 10 minutes, or until firm.

3 Preheat the oven to 500 degrees F.

4 In a small bowl, combine the garlic and oil. Set aside for about 15 minutes to allow the garlic to infuse the oil.

5 When the polenta is firm, cut it into 6 rectangles or squares of equal size. Slice each shape diagonally into 4 triangles. Brush each triangle very lightly with the garlic-infused oil and lay on a nonstick baking sheet. Sprinkle the rosemary leaves on top and push a few underneath each triangle. Gently push down on the rosemary so that the leaves adhere to the polenta. Season with pepper to taste.

6 Bake in the top half of the oven for 7 to 10 minutes, or until very crisp on the outside but still soft in the center. Serve hot.

NOTE: Sally recommends that you use the traditional coarsely milled cornmeal available in Italian markets or specialty food shops for polenta, as it has a more interesting texture and a more robust flavor than finely grained polenta flours.

GORDON HAMERSLEY

Braised Wild Mushrooms with Roasted Garlic Toasts

SERVES 6
PREPARATION TIME: ABOUT 15 MINUTES
COOKING TIME: ABOUT 18 MINUTES

FAT PER SERVING: 3.5 GRAMS
SATURATED FAT: 0.9 GRAM
CALORIES PER SERVING: 147
CALORIES FROM FAT: 20%

So simple, light, and easy to prepare, yet this quick braise is full of robust flavor. Having roasted garlic on hand turns this into a meal in a minute! Double the recipe for a terrific brunch or late-night supper dish.

1 pound fresh wild mushrooms in any combination (shiitakes, chanterelles, cremini, pleurottes, porcinis, morels, and/or oysters)
2 1/2 teaspoons olive oil
3 shallots, minced
2 cloves garlic, minced
Pinch of dried thyme or marjoram
1/4 cup dry white wine
Coarse salt and freshly ground black pepper to taste
1 teaspoon unsalted butter (optional)
Six 1/4-inch-thick slices French bread
1/4 cup plus 2 tablespoons Roasted Garlic pulp (see page 15)
6 sprigs watercress, for garnish

1 Assemble *mise en place* trays for this recipe (see page 6). Preheat the oven to 350 degrees F.

2 Using a damp cloth, wipe the mushrooms clean. Trim off any tough stems and cut the larger mushrooms in half. In a large sauté pan, heat 1 1/2 teaspoons of the oil over medium-high heat. Add the mushrooms and sauté for about 3 minutes, or until the mushrooms begin to exude their juices. Stir in the shallots, garlic, and herbs. Add the wine and coarse salt and pepper to taste and bring to a simmer. Lower the heat and simmer gently for about 5 minutes, or until the mushrooms are tender and the juices have thickened slightly. Stir in the butter, if desired, until smooth and melted.

3 Brush the bread on one side with the remaining 1 teaspoon oil and sprinkle with coarse salt and pepper to taste. Lay on a baking sheet and bake for about 5 minutes, or until lightly toasted. Spread 1 tablespoon garlic pulp on each slice and bake for about 3 more minutes, until the croutons are browned.

4 Place 1 hot crouton on each of 6 warm plates or in each of 6 shallow soup bowls. Top with the mushroom ragout and garnish with the watercress.

GORDON HAMERSLEY

Asparagus Salad with Littleneck Clams and Thyme

SERVES 6
PREPARATION TIME: ABOUT 30 MINUTES
COOKING TIME: ABOUT 15 MINUTES

FAT PER SERVING: 5.5 GRAMS
SATURATED FAT: 0.7 GRAM
CALORIES PER SERVING: 159
CALORIES FROM FAT: 35%

Elegant, but so light and easy to prepare, this salad makes an excellent dinner party first course, or double the recipe for a beautiful luncheon main course. The percentage of fat looks high here, but note that there are only 159 calories and 5.5 grams of fat per serving.

2 tablespoons plus 2 teaspoons olive oil, or more if desired
2 shallots, minced
2 cloves garlic, sliced

18 littleneck clams, scrubbed
1 cup dry white wine
1/2 teaspoon chopped fresh thyme
Pinch of fennel seeds
Pinch of red pepper flakes
Juice of 1 lemon
1 teaspoon Dijon mustard
Coarse salt and freshly ground black pepper to taste
24 spears asparagus, trimmed and blanched
6 sprigs watercress, for garnish
Six 1/2-inch-thick slices French bread, toasted

1 Assemble *mise en place* trays for this recipe (see page 6).

2 Set a sauté pan large enough to hold the clams in a single layer over medium heat and heat 1 teaspoon of the oil. When hot but not smoking, add the shallots and garlic and sauté for 1 minute. Stir in the clams, wine, thyme, fennel seeds, and red pepper flakes. Cover and cook for about 5 minutes, or just until the clams start to open. Using a slotted spoon, remove the clams to a bowl, cover, and refrigerate; discard any that have not opened. Simmer the liquid for about 5 minutes longer, or until reduced by half. Allow to cool to room temperature.

3 Whisk the lemon juice and mustard into the cooled liquid. Add 2 tablespoons olive oil in a slow, steady stream, whisking constantly until well emulsified. Add additional oil if desired to make a thick vinaigrette. Season to taste with coarse salt and pepper. Set aside.

4 Divide the remaining 1 teaspoon oil between 2 sauté pans and heat over medium heat. Add the clams to one pan and the asparagus to the other. Using tongs, gently rotate the clams and asparagus just until heated through.

5 Place a piece of toast on each warm plate. Crisscross 4 asparagus spears on top of each and top with the clams. Drizzle the dressing over the clams, garnish each plate with a sprig of watercress, and serve immediately.

NOTE: Any shellfish could replace the clams in this recipe. If you prefer, remove the clams from their shells before reheating them.

MARIO BATALI
Asparagus and Morel Bruschetta

SERVES 6
PREPARATION TIME: ABOUT 15 MINUTES
COOKING TIME: ABOUT 10 MINUTES

FAT PER SERVING: 5.5 GRAMS
SATURATED FAT: 0.8 GRAM
CALORIES PER SERVING: 195
CALORIES FROM FAT: 25%

The flavors of spring absolutely sing through this aromatic mixture. It could also be served on a bed of wild greens for a first-course salad. Tossed with pasta, it's a delicious main course.

2 teaspoons olive oil
3 shallots, minced
6 ounces fresh morels, trimmed
10 medium-sized spears asparagus (about 1/2 pound), trimmed, blanched, and cut into 1/4-inch pieces
Juice of 1 small lemon
3 tablespoons fresh thyme leaves
1 tablespoon extra-virgin olive oil
1 tablespoon white truffle oil (optional)
Coarse salt and freshly ground black pepper to taste
Twenty-four 1/4-inch-thick slices French bread, toasted

1 Assemble *mise en place* trays for this recipe (see page 6).

2 In a medium-sized sauté pan, heat the 2 teaspoons olive oil over medium heat. Add the shallots and cook for 1 minute. Add the morels and sauté for about 5 minutes, or until tender. Remove from the heat. Add the asparagus, lemon juice, thyme, extra-virgin olive oil, and the truffle oil if desired. Toss gently and season to taste with coarse salt and pepper.

3 Place 3 slices of toast on each warm plate. Spoon the morel mixture onto the toast and serve immediately.

NOTE: You can replace the morels, which are very expensive, with any other aromatic wild mushrooms, such as cremini, shiitakes, or chanterelles.

▶ **White truffle oil is available at specialty food markets.**

◁ **GORDON HAMERSLEY:** *(top)* Braised Wild Mushrooms with Roasted Garlic Toasts; *(bottom)* Asparagus Salad with Littleneck Clams and Thyme

MARIE SIMMONS
Smothered Escarole on Whole Wheat Crostini

SERVES 6
PREPARATION TIME: ABOUT 20 MINUTES
COOKING TIME: ABOUT 10 MINUTES

FAT PER SERVING: 3 GRAMS
SATURATED FAT: 0.4 GRAM
CALORIES PER SERVING: 83
CALORIES FROM FAT: 32%

(top) **MARIO BATALI:** Asparagus and Morel Bruschetta; *(bottom)* **MARIE SIMMONS:** Smothered Escarole on Whole Wheat Crostini

Rich in vitamins and slightly bitter, escarole makes a crunchy, easy-to-prepare appetizer. You could use other greens in its place, but try to use whole wheat bread: Its sweetness offsets the greens beautifully.

2 pounds escarole, washed, trimmed, and torn into 2-inch pieces
1 tablespoon extra-virgin olive oil
1 clove garlic, crushed
Pinch of red pepper flakes
Coarse salt and freshly ground black pepper to taste
Twelve ¼-inch-thick slices whole wheat Italian bread, toasted

1 Assemble *mise en place* trays for this recipe (see page 6).

2 Bring a large saucepan of water to a boil over high heat. Add the escarole and cook, stirring constantly with a wooden spoon, for about 4 minutes, or until just tender. Drain in a colander, pressing on the escarole with the back of the spoon to remove all moisture. Set aside.

3 In a large sauté pan, combine the oil, garlic, and red pepper flakes and cook over medium-low heat for about 3 minutes, or until the garlic begins to sizzle. Immediately add the escarole and stir to coat. Cook, stirring constantly, for about 2 minutes, or until the pan juices begin to evaporate. Season to taste with coarse salt and pepper.

4 Place 2 slices of toast on each warm plate. Spoon the escarole over the toast and serve immediately.

▶ Whole wheat Italian bread makes especially delicious crostini, or toasts. Use a grill, broiler, or toaster oven. Brush the bread with olive oil and toast until golden on both sides. To prepare crostini in the oven, brush the bread very lightly on one side with olive oil and lay on a baking sheet. Bake in a preheated 350-degree-F oven for about 15 minutes, or until the edges are golden. If desired, rub the toasted bread very lightly with the cut side of a halved garlic clove. You can also bake split pita-bread crostini in the same fashion.

▶ Escarole prepared this way is also a delicious side dish served with chicken, veal, or fish.

PATRICIA JAMIESON
Caramelized Onion Pizza

SERVES 6
PREPARATION TIME: ABOUT 1 HOUR
COOKING TIME: ABOUT 1 HOUR AND 5
  MINUTES

FAT PER SERVING: 12 GRAMS
SATURATED FAT: 2.9 GRAMS
CALORIES PER PIZZA: 295
CALORIES FROM FAT: 23%

The rosemary and olives in the dough give these pizzas an earthy flavor, while the onions add rich sweetness. Cut into wedges, these make great appetizers. Left whole, they are an excellent lunch or late-night snack. The dough recipe makes enough for eight pizzas, which means you can freeze some for another time.

1½ teaspoons olive oil
4 cups sliced onions (about 4 medium-sized onions)
Coarse salt and freshly ground black pepper to taste
1 tablespoon balsamic vinegar
1 recipe Quick-Rising Pizza Dough (recipe follows)
¾ cup (about ¼ pound) Kalamata or Gaeta olives, pitted and chopped
1 tablespoon chopped fresh rosemary or 1 teaspoon crumbled dried
About 1 cup yellow or white cornmeal
¾ cup grated part-skim-milk mozzarella cheese (about 3 ounces)

■ Special Equipment: Pizza stone or baking tiles; pizza peel

1 Assemble *mise en place* trays for this recipe (see page 6).

2 In a large nonstick sauté pan, heat the oil over medium-low heat. Add the onions, season to taste with coarse salt and pepper, and cook, stirring frequently, for about 20 minutes, or until lightly browned and soft. Stir in the vinegar. Taste and adjust the seasoning with salt and pepper. Set aside to cool.

3 Place a pizza stone, baking tiles, or an inverted heavy-duty baking sheet on the lowest rack of the oven. Preheat the oven to 500 degrees F (or the highest setting).

4 Place the dough on a lightly floured surface and knead in the olives and rosemary. When evenly incorporated, divide the dough into 8 equal pieces. Wrap 2 pieces in wax paper and then in plastic wrap and freeze for a later use.

5 Using your fists, stretch 2 pieces of the dough into 6-inch circles. As you work, keep the remaining dough covered with a kitchen towel or plastic wrap. Put the rounds side by side on a cornmeal-dusted pizza peel or inverted baking sheet, using enough cornmeal so that the dough will slide easily off the peel. Working with 2 pieces of dough at a time, continue to make circles as described above. (Alternatively, use a rolling pin to roll out, on a lightly floured surface, into 6-inch circles.)

6 Sprinkle 2 tablespoons of mozzarella over each dough circle and arrange about ¼ cup of the onions on top of each. Carefully slide the pizzas onto the hot stone in the oven and bake for about 14 minutes, or until the bottoms are crisp and well browned. Serve hot or at room temperature.

NOTE: If you have more than one oven, you can bake 4 pizzas at the same time. Do not bake more than 2 at a time in each oven, as the pizzas must bake on the hot tiles.

QUICK-RISING PIZZA DOUGH
MAKES ENOUGH FOR EIGHT 6-INCH PIZZAS

1¾ cups water
2 teaspoons olive oil
4 to 4½ cups all-purpose flour
Two ¼-ounce packages rapid-rise yeast
2 teaspoons salt
1 teaspoon granulated sugar

■ Special Equipment: Candy thermometer

1 In a small saucepan, heat the water and oil over low heat until the mixture reaches a temperature of 125 degrees F on a candy thermometer. Remove from the heat.

2 In a large bowl, stir together 3 cups flour, the yeast, salt, and sugar. Using a wooden spoon, gradually stir in the water mixture until well mixed. Slowly add enough of the remaining flour to make a firm, soft dough. Turn out onto a lightly floured surface and knead for 8 to 10 minutes, until smooth and elastic. Cover with plastic wrap and let rest for 10 minutes, then roll out as directed in the recipe.

NOTE: Alternatively, in a large-capacity food processor fitted with the metal blade, combine 4 cups flour, the yeast,

salt, and sugar. With the motor running, gradually pour 1½ cups warm water (125 degrees F) and 2 teaspoons olive oil through the feed tube. Process, adding up to 2 tablespoons cold water if necessary, until the dough forms a ball, then process for 1 minute to knead. Turn out onto a lightly floured surface, cover with plastic wrap, and let rest for 10 minutes.

▶ Rapid-rise is a strain of yeast that does not need to be dissolved separately in liquid. It requires only a 10-minute resting time instead of the traditional 1- to 2-hour rise. Look for Fleishmann's Rapid-Rise Yeast in the supermarket.

▶ The dough can be made ahead, enclosed in a large plastic bag, and stored in the refrigerator overnight. Bring to room temperature before using.

JANE BRODY: Intercontinental Chickpea Spread *and*
PATRICIA JAMIESON: Caramelized Onion Pizza

JANE BRODY
Intercontinental Chickpea Spread

SERVES 6
PREPARATION TIME: ABOUT 30 MINUTES
CHILLING TIME: ABOUT 1 HOUR

FAT PER SERVING: 9 GRAMS
SATURATED FAT: 2.8 GRAMS
CALORIES PER SERVING: 237
CALORIES FROM FAT: 35%

Jane told us that this spread is always a tremendous hit at gatherings. All the ingredients can be prepared ahead of time but, if the spread is prepared more than an hour or so before serving, it may get runny. The percentage of fat is relatively high, but the saturated fat is quite low. The spread can be scooped up with toasted pita wedges, baked tortilla chips, or crisp raw vegetables.

One 20-ounce can chickpeas, rinsed and drained
¼ cup plain nonfat yogurt
1 large clove garlic, chopped
½ teaspoon salt, or to taste
⅓ cup store-bought salsa, preferably hot
1 small zucchini, shredded and squeezed almost dry (about ½ cup before squeezing)
3 ripe plum tomatoes, peeled, seeded, drained, and cut into small dice
2 tablespoons diced red onion
2 tablespoons shredded Parmigiano-Reggiano cheese
1 tablespoon chopped fresh cilantro

1 Assemble *mise en place* trays for this recipe (see page 6).

2 Combine the chickpeas, yogurt, garlic, and salt in a food processor fitted with the metal blade and process to a smooth paste. Transfer to a container, cover, and refrigerate for about 1 hour, or until well chilled.

DOUGLAS RODRIGUEZ
Shrimp Ceviche

SERVES 6
PREPARATION TIME: ABOUT 30 MINUTES
COOKING TIME: ABOUT 2 MINUTES
CHILLING TIME: AT LEAST 1 HOUR

FAT PER SERVING: 1.4 GRAMS
SATURATED FAT: 0.2 GRAM
CALORIES PER SERVING: 113
CALORIES FROM FAT: 11%

This recipe is Doug Rodriguez at his best. He is well known for light, refreshing, perfectly flavored ceviches finished with absolutely wild garnishes. This one will not disappoint.

1½ pounds medium shrimp, peeled and deveined
2 red bell peppers, roasted, peeled, cored, and seeded (see page 12)
2 jalapeño chiles, roasted, peeled, cored, and seeded (see page 12)
1 large tomato, roasted, peeled, cored, and seeded (see page 12)
1 small onion, roasted and chopped (see page 12)
¾ cup fresh lime juice (5 to 6 limes)
½ cup fresh orange juice
¼ cup tomato juice
1 scant tablespoon granulated sugar
Tabasco sauce to taste
Salt to taste
1 small red onion, sliced
1 large tomato, peeled, cored, seeded, and finely diced
2 tablespoons chopped scallions, white part only
2 tablespoons chopped fresh chives
About 15 fresh cilantro leaves
1 cup unsalted popcorn
½ cup corn nuts

1 Assemble *mise en place* trays for this recipe (see page 6).

2 Bring a large saucepan of water to a boil. Add the shrimp and cook for 2 minutes, or just until pink and opaque throughout. Drain and place in an ice water bath to stop the cooking. Drain, pat dry, and put in a nonreactive container.

3 Just before serving, put the chickpea spread on a chilled plate and pour the salsa over it. Sprinkle with the zucchini, tomatoes, onions, cheese, and cilantro and serve immediately.

▶ **Although this recipe calls for prepared salsa, if you have the time, by all means make it fresh.**

3 In a blender, combine the roasted vegetables, the lime, orange and tomato juices, the sugar, and Tabasco and salt to taste. Process until smooth and pour over the shrimp. Cover and refrigerate for at least 1 hour, or until chilled.

4 When ready to serve, toss the shrimp mixture with the sliced onion, chopped tomato, scallions, chives, and cilantro. Mound on chilled plates, sprinkle with the popcorn and corn nuts, and serve immediately.

DOUG RODRIGUEZ: Shrimp Ceviche

MARIE SIMMONS
Chilled Curried Tomato Soup with Cilantro Cream

SERVES 6
PREPARATION TIME: ABOUT 30 MINUTES
COOKING TIME: ABOUT 25 MINUTES
CHILLING TIME: AT LEAST 1 HOUR

FAT PER SERVING: 6.9 GRAMS
SATURATED FAT: 1.7 GRAMS
CALORIES PER SERVING: 210
CALORIES FROM FAT: 29%

This cool soup is made creamy with the addition of the cilantro topping. You can make the soup with either whole-milk or low-fat yogurt and whole or low-fat milk (if needed). (The nutritional analysis is based on low-fat yogurt and skim milk.) Marie feels the Cilantro Cream is best made with low-fat yogurt. You could leave the herb cream out completely to cut the fat and calories.

2 tablespoons olive oil
1¹/2 cups finely chopped onions
3 cloves garlic, minced
1 to 1¹/2 tablespoons curry powder, or to taste
One-and-one-half 35-ounce boxes strained tomatoes (about 6¹/2 cups, see Note)
3 cups plain low-fat yogurt, at room temperature, stirred until smooth
Salt and freshly ground black pepper to taste
¹/4 cup milk, if needed
Cilantro Cream (recipe follows)

1 Assemble *mise en place* trays for this recipe (see page 6).

2 In a large saucepan, combine the oil and onions and cook over low heat, stirring frequently, for about 5 minutes, or until the onions are soft and golden. Add the garlic and curry powder to taste and cook, stirring constantly, for 1 minute. Stir in the tomatoes, cover, and cook for about 15 minutes, or until the flavors are well blended. Uncover and let cool to lukewarm.

3 Transfer to a food processor fitted with the metal blade and process until smooth. (This may have to be done in batches.) Transfer to a nonreactive bowl and whisk in the yogurt and salt and pepper to taste. Cover and refrigerate for at least 1 hour, or until chilled.

4 If necessary, thin the soup by whisking in the milk, a little at a time. Pour into chilled shallow soup bowls. Swirl a dollop of Cilantro Cream into each serving and serve immediately.

NOTE: Pomi brand produces excellent boxed strained tomatoes.

CILANTRO CREAM

MAKES ABOUT 1 CUP
FAT PER 2¹/2-TABLESPOON SERVING: 1.9 GRAMS
SATURATED FAT: 1.1 GRAMS
CALORIES PER SERVING: 31
CALORIES FROM FAT: 59%

¹/2 cup plain low-fat yogurt
2 tablespoons heavy cream (optional)
¹/2 cup packed fresh cilantro leaves

Combine the yogurt, cream, and cilantro in a food processor fitted with the metal blade and process until smooth. Transfer to a container, cover, and refrigerate for at least 1 hour, or until well chilled.

◁ MARIE SIMMONS: Chilled Curried Tomato Soup with Cilantro Cream

SHEILA LUKINS
Sweet Pepper and Yellow Pepper Soup

SERVES 6
PREPARATION TIME: ABOUT 35 MINUTES
COOKING TIME: ABOUT 45 MINUTES

FAT PER SERVING: 5.2 GRAMS
SATURATED FAT: 2.4 GRAMS
CALORIES PER SERVING: 190
CALORIES FROM FAT: 23%

The richly colored red and yellow peppers are used to make two separate soups that, when combined, form a dish that is as good to eat as it is pretty to behold. For the presentation, the two soups are simultaneously poured down opposite sides of a shallow bowl. This is remarkably easy to do and makes an impressive dinner party first course.

2 red bell peppers, cored, seeded, and cut into ¼-inch-thick strips
10 very ripe plum tomatoes, cored, quartered, and seeded
¼ cup fresh lemon juice
½ teaspoon ground ginger
¼ teaspoon freshly ground black pepper, plus more to taste
Salt to taste
2 tablespoons unsalted butter
1 cup chopped onions
1 cup chopped leeks
6 yellow bell peppers, 3 roasted, peeled, cored, seeded, and chopped (see page 12) and 3 cored, seeded, and chopped
3 small boiling potatoes (about ¾ pound), peeled and sliced
5 cups Chicken Stock (see page 14)
2 tablespoons chopped fresh chives, for garnish

1 Assemble *mise en place* trays for this recipe (see page 6).

2 In a large heavy saucepan, combine the red peppers, tomatoes, lemon juice, ginger, and ¼ teaspoon pepper and bring to a simmer over low heat. Cover and cook, stirring occasionally, for about 30 minutes, or until the peppers are very soft.

3 Transfer to a food processor fitted with the metal blade and process until smooth. Taste and adjust the seasoning with salt and pepper. (You may have to do this in batches.) Pour into a medium-sized saucepan and set aside.

4 Meanwhile, make the yellow pepper soup: In a large saucepan, melt the butter over low heat. Add the onions and leeks and season to taste with salt and pepper. Cook,

SHEILA LUKINS: Sweet Pepper and Yellow Pepper Soup

stirring frequently, for about 15 minutes, or until the vegetables are tender and translucent. Add the yellow peppers, potatoes, and stock. Raise the heat and bring to a boil, then reduce the heat and simmer for about 30 minutes, or until the vegetables are very tender.

5 Transfer to a food processor fitted with the metal blade and process until smooth. (You may have to do this in batches.) Pour into a medium-sized saucepan, taste, and adjust the seasoning.

6 Heat both soups over medium heat, stirring frequently, for about 3 minutes, or until just heated through.

7 Fill a measuring cup with a portion of one soup and fill another with the other soup. Slowly pour one soup down one side of a shallow soup bowl while simultaneously pouring the other soup down the opposite side, so that they meet in the middle of the bowl. Fill 5 more bowls the same way, garnish with the chives, and serve immediately.

NOTE: Either of these soups can be served alone. The yellow pepper soup is superb with a splash of extra-virgin olive oil, a grating of Parmesan cheese, and crisp croutons.

▶ Replace the homemade chicken stock with canned low-sodium chicken broth if desired.

MARK MILITELLO

Chilled Summer Vegetable Soup with Spanish Vinegar and Quinoa Salad

SERVES 6
PREPARATION TIME: ABOUT 45 MINUTES
COOKING TIME: ABOUT 45 MINUTES
CHILLING TIME: AT LEAST 3 HOURS

FAT PER SERVING: 10 GRAMS
SATURATED FAT: 1.2 GRAMS
CALORIES PER SERVING: 347
CALORIES FROM FAT: 25%

This soup is a meal in itself! The rich vegetable flavor is enhanced by a touch of vinegar and extended by the grain salad. This is a masterpiece of low-fat cooking.

2 tablespoons olive oil, plus more for garnish if desired
1/2 pound sweet onions, such as Vidalia, diced
3/4 pound tomatoes, peeled, cored, and quartered
3/4 pound red bell peppers, cored, seeded, and diced
1/2 pound baking potatoes, peeled and diced
1/2 pound eggplant, diced
1/2 pound zucchini, diced
2 cloves garlic, chopped
1 small bunch each fresh thyme, basil, and flat-leaf parsley, tied together in a cheesecloth bag
4 cups Chicken Stock (see page 14)
Salt and freshly ground black pepper to taste
About 2 tablespoons Spanish vinegar, such as L'Estornell
Quinoa Salad (recipe follows)
1 small piece Parmigiano-Reggiano cheese, for shaving (optional)

▪ Special Equipment: Food mill

1 Assemble *mise en place* trays for this recipe (see page 6).

2 In a large saucepan, heat the oil over medium heat. Add the onions and sauté for about 5 minutes, or until soft but not brown. Add the tomatoes, bell peppers, potatoes, eggplant, zucchini, garlic, herb bundle, and stock. Raise the heat and bring to a boil, then reduce the heat and simmer for about 30 minutes, or until the vegetables are soft. Pass the vegetables through the medium-sized plate of a food mill into a nonreactive container. Season with salt and pepper to taste, cover, cool, and refrigerate for at least 3 hours, or until chilled.

3 When ready to serve, stir vinegar to taste into the soup.

4 For each serving, spoon Quinoa Salad into a 1/2-cup mold and invert the molds into the center of a large shallow soup bowl. Ladle equal portions of soup around the salads. If desired, drizzle oil onto the soup and shave a bit of Parmesan on top. Serve immediately.

NOTE: Chop each vegetable into equal-sized pieces so that they cook uniformly.

MARK MILITELLO: Chilled Summer Vegetable Soup with Spanish Vinegar and Quinoa Salad

QUINOA SALAD

$^1/_2$ cup quinoa, rinsed
1 cup water
$^1/_2$ cup finely diced seeded cucumber
$^1/_2$ cup peas, blanched
$^1/_2$ cup corn kernels, blanched
$^1/_4$ cup finely diced fennel
$^1/_4$ cup finely diced celery
$^1/_4$ cup chopped fresh basil
2 tablespoons chopped fresh mint
$^1/_4$ cup fresh lemon juice, or more to taste
1 tablespoon extra-virgin olive oil
Sea salt and freshly ground black pepper to taste

1 In a medium-sized saucepan, combine the quinoa and water and bring to a boil over high heat. Reduce the heat and simmer for about 10 minutes, or until all the water has been absorbed and the quinoa is tender. Set aside to cool.

2 In a nonreactive bowl, combine the cucumber, peas, corn, fennel, celery, herbs, lemon juice, and oil. Add the quinoa, toss, and season to taste with sea salt and pepper. Cover and marinate at room temperature for 1 hour to allow the flavors to develop.

3 Just before serving, adjust the seasoning with extra lemon juice, salt, and/or pepper if necessary.

NOTE: You will have more than enough salad to garnish the soup, which you can serve as a side dish or with greens for another meal. Store, covered and refrigerated, for up to 2 days.

DANIEL BOULUD

Eggplant and Crab Garbure with Cumin and Tomato Confit

SERVES 6
PREPARATION TIME: ABOUT 1 HOUR
COOKING TIME: ABOUT 40 MINUTES

FAT PER SERVING: 10 GRAMS
SATURATED FAT: 1.2 GRAMS
CALORIES PER SERVING: 166
CALORIES FROM FAT: 25%

Garbure is an earthy vegetable soup from the southwest of France. In this recipe, Daniel replaces the fat and flavor of the traditional bacon and goose confit with crab and a tomato confit.

1 tablespoon salt, plus more to taste
3 medium-sized eggplant, peeled and cut into thin 1-inch-long strips (avoiding the seedy center)
1 tablespoon olive oil
1½ cups sliced onions (¼ inch thick)
1½ cups sliced leeks (¼ inch thick)
1½ cups thinly sliced carrots
2 cloves garlic, minced
2 bay leaves
2 sprigs fresh thyme
2 teaspoons ground cumin
½ teaspoon ground coriander
8 cups warm Chicken Stock (see page 14)
Freshly ground black pepper to taste
¾ cup jumbo lump crabmeat, picked over for shells and cartilage
Tomato Confit (recipe follows)
6 sprigs fresh chervil, for garnish

1 Assemble *mise en place* trays for this recipe (see page 6).

2 In a large saucepan, bring 2 quarts of water to boil over high heat. Add the 1 tablespoon salt and the eggplant and cook for about 3 minutes, or until the eggplant is slightly softened. Drain and set aside.

3 In a medium-sized saucepan, heat the oil over medium heat. Add the onions, leeks, carrots, garlic, herbs, cumin, and coriander and sauté for about 6 minutes, or until the vegetables are just soft. Add the stock, blanched eggplant, and salt and pepper to taste, and simmer for about 25 minutes, or until the vegetables are very tender.

4 Remove the bay leaves and thyme sprigs. Gently stir in the crab and then ladle into shallow soup bowls. Gently float the pieces of tomato confit on top of the soup and put a chervil sprig in the center of each. Serve immediately.

NOTE: Cut the vegetables into equal-sized pieces so that they cook uniformly. The soup can be made up to the addition of the crab up to 3 days ahead. If fresh chervil is not available, use flat-leaf parsley.

TOMATO CONFIT

4 plum tomatoes, peeled, cored, quartered, and seeded
1 large clove garlic, quartered
1 teaspoon ground cumin
½ teaspoon ground coriander
2 teaspoons olive oil
Salt and freshly ground black pepper to taste

1 Preheat the oven to 350 degrees F.

2 Lay the tomatoes in a small baking pan and sprinkle them with the garlic, spices, oil, and salt and pepper to taste. Bake for about 10 minutes, or until the tomatoes soften. Remove and discard the garlic. Use immediately, or set aside until ready to serve. If necessary, reheat over very low heat just until warm.

NOTE: The confit can be made up to 1 week ahead, covered, and refrigerated. Bring to room temperature and heat just until warm before serving.

(See pages 16–17 for photograph)

Salads and Side Dishes

Gingered Green Bean Salad

Appaloosa, Butterscotch, and Chestnut Bean Salad

Parsley Salad with Bulgur, Mint, and Tomatoes

Wild Rice-Orzo Pilaf

Roasted Sweet Potatoes

Couscous and Sautéed Savoy Cabbage

Potato Shoes

Roasted Onions with Mustard Vinaigrette

JANE BRODY
Gingered Green Bean Salad

SERVES 6
PREPARATION TIME: ABOUT 15 MINUTES
COOKING TIME: ABOUT 5 MINUTES
CHILLING TIME: AT LEAST 30 MINUTES

FAT PER SERVING: 7.4 GRAMS
SATURATED FAT: 0.7 GRAM
CALORIES PER SERVING: 107
CALORIES FROM FAT: 56%

(ANALYSIS WITHOUT ALMONDS)
FAT PER SERVING: 1.7 GRAMS
SATURATED FAT: 0.2 GRAM
CALORIES PER SERVING: 42
CALORIES FROM FAT: 34%

This wholesome salad with an Asian twist is made without oil. It has the added virtue of keeping, covered and refrigerated, for up to five days. To cut back on the fat, omit the almonds, or use half the amount.

1 pound green beans, trimmed and cut into 2-inch-long pieces
1 tablespoon finely shredded fresh ginger
1/3 cup sliced blanched almonds
1 to 2 teaspoons dry mustard, or to taste
About 1 1/2 teaspoons water
1 teaspoon granulated sugar
1 1/2 tablespoons distilled white vinegar or rice vinegar
1 tablespoon reduced-sodium soy sauce
1 teaspoon salt, or to taste (optional)

1 Assemble *mise en place* trays for this recipe (see page 6).

2 In the top half of a vegetable steamer set over boiling water, steam the beans for about 5 minutes, or until just tender. Rinse under cold running water and pat dry.

3 In a medium bowl, combine the beans, ginger, and almonds.

4 In a small bowl, whisk together the mustard and water to make a paste. Stir in the sugar, vinegar, soy sauce, and, if using, the salt. Pour over the bean mixture and toss to coat. Cover and refrigerate for at least 30 minutes before serving.

NOTE: Do not substitute powdered ginger for fresh ginger. Fresh ginger is readily available in supermarkets and greengrocers.

(See pages 34–35 for photograph)

RON HOOK
Appaloosa, Butterscotch, and Chestnut Bean Salad

SERVES 6
PREPARATION TIME: ABOUT 30 MINUTES
COOKING TIME: ABOUT 40 MINUTES
SOAKING TIME: 1 HOUR
CHILLING TIME: AT LEAST 2 HOURS

FAT PER SERVING: 0.4 GRAM
SATURATED FAT: 0.1 GRAM
CALORIES PER SERVING: 87
CALORIES FROM FAT: 4%

This hearty salad is deliciously heart-healthy: Low in fat and cholesterol, it's filled with tasty goodness. Serve it as a side dish or a casual main course.

1/2 cup each Appaloosa, butterscotch, and chestnut beans, rinsed and picked clean (see Note)
1 bay leaf
1/2 cup fresh lemon juice
1/4 cup balsamic vinegar
2 tablespoons Roasted Garlic pulp (see page 15)
3 large fresh sage leaves
1/2 teaspoon coarse salt
1/2 teaspoon freshly ground black pepper
1 medium onion, thinly sliced
3 tablespoons finely grated carrot
1 tablespoon chopped fresh flat-leaf parsley
1 head red-leaf lettuce, separated into leaves, washed, and dried

1 Assemble *mise en place* trays for this recipe (see page 6).

2 In a large saucepan, combine the beans with water to cover by 1 to 2 inches and bring to a boil over high heat. Immediately remove the pan from the heat and let stand for 1 hour.

3 Drain the beans, rinse, and cover with fresh cold water. Add the bay leaf and bring to a boil over high heat. Reduce the heat and simmer for about 40 minutes, or until the beans are tender. Drain and discard the bay leaf. Transfer to a heat-proof bowl.

(See page 45 for photograph)

4 In a blender, combine the lemon juice, vinegar, garlic, sage, and coarse salt and pepper. Add ¼ cup of the cooked beans and process until smooth. Pour over the remaining warm beans and toss to coat. Stir in the onion, 2 tablespoons of the carrot, and the parsley. Cover and refrigerate for at least 2 hours.

5 Arrange the lettuce leaves in a circle around the edge of a serving plate. Pile the bean salad in the center, sprinkle the remaining 1 tablespoon grated carrot on top, and serve immediately.

NOTE: You can use any combination of dried beans to make this salad. However, try to use those that have a good color balance, such as kidney, cranberry, and white beans.

CHRIS SCHLESINGER
Parsley Salad with Bulgur, Mint, and Tomatoes

SERVES 6
PREPARATION TIME: ABOUT 20 MINUTES
SOAKING TIME: 30 MINUTES

FAT PER SERVING: 1.6 GRAMS
SATURATED FAT: 0.5 GRAM
CALORIES PER SERVING: 89
CALORIES FROM FAT: 15%

This is Chris's version of the traditional Middle Eastern salad called tabbouleh. You can make it with any size bulgur grain, but medium-fine gives the best result.

⅓ cup medium-fine bulgur, rinsed
1 cup water
3 tomatoes, peeled, cored, seeded, and finely diced
1 red onion, finely diced
1 cucumber, peeled and finely diced
3 cups finely chopped fresh flat-leaf parsley
¼ cup finely chopped fresh mint
1 teaspoon minced garlic
½ cup fresh lemon juice (about 3 lemons)
⅓ cup extra-virgin olive oil
2 to 6 drops Tabasco sauce
Salt to taste
1 head romaine lettuce, separated into leaves, washed, and dried

1 Assemble *mise en place* trays for this recipe (see page 6).

2 In a bowl, combine the bulgur and water, cover, and set aside for 30 minutes. Drain in a fine sieve and use your hands to squeeze out any excess water. Transfer to a large bowl.

3 Add the tomatoes, onions, cucumber, parsley, mint, garlic, lemon juice, oil, and Tabasco and salt to taste. Serve immediately, or cover and refrigerate for up to 4 hours. Bring to room temperature before serving. Use the lettuce leaves for scooping up and eating the salad.

CHRIS SCHLESINGER: Parsley Salad with Bulgur, Mint, and Tomatoes

NOTE: Do not make this more than 4 hours in advance, or the vegetables will get soggy.

PATRICIA JAMIESON
Wild Rice-Orzo Pilaf

SERVES 6
PREPARATION TIME: ABOUT 20 MINUTES
COOKING TIME: ABOUT 50 MINUTES

FAT PER SERVING: 6.7 GRAMS
SATURATED FAT: 0.5 GRAM
CALORIES PER SERVING: 244
CALORIES FROM FAT: 24%

Aromatic wild rice gives a rich and flavorful dimension to this pilaf. It is a particularly festive side dish for entertaining or the holidays, with the added bonus that it can be prepared ahead of time.

2 teaspoons vegetable oil
1 large onion, chopped
1 rib celery, finely chopped
1¼ cups wild rice, rinsed
2¾ cups Chicken Stock (see page 14), heated to boiling
1 sprig fresh thyme or ½ teaspoon dried
½ cup orzo
2 tablespoons finely chopped scallions
2 tablespoons finely chopped fresh flat-leaf parsley
1 teaspoon grated orange zest
Salt and freshly ground black pepper to taste
¼ cup chopped toasted pecans or almonds, for garnish (optional)

1 Assemble *mise en place* trays for this recipe (see page 6).

2 In a large heavy saucepan, heat the oil over medium heat. Add the onions and celery and sauté for about 5 minutes, or until the vegetables soften. Stir in the wild rice. Add the stock and thyme and bring to a simmer. Reduce the heat to medium-low, cover, and cook gently for about 50 minutes, or until the rice is tender and all the liquid is absorbed.

3 Meanwhile, cook the orzo in a medium-sized saucepan of boiling barely salted water for about 7 minutes, or until just tender. Drain in a sieve and rinse under warm running water.

4 Stir the orzo, scallions, parsley, and zest into the rice. Season to taste with salt and pepper. Put in a serving bowl, garnish with the nuts if desired, and serve immediately.

NOTE: The pilaf can be made up to 2 days ahead, covered, and refrigerated. To reheat, place in a casserole sprayed with nonstick vegetable spray. Cover and bake in a preheated 325-degree-F oven for about 20 minutes, until heated through.

(See page 50 for photograph)

PATRICIA JAMIESON
Roasted Sweet Potatoes

SERVES 6
PREPARATION TIME: ABOUT 10 MINUTES
ROASTING TIME: ABOUT 15 MINUTES

FAT PER SERVING: 2.3 GRAMS
SATURATED FAT: 0.3 GRAM
CALORIES PER SERVING: 108
CALORIES FROM FAT: 19%

These are a healthy alternative to the traditional holiday sweet potato casserole. They are so good you will find them to be almost addictive at any time of the year.

2 medium-sized sweet potatoes, peeled and cut into ¼-inch-thick slices
1 tablespoon olive oil
Salt and freshly ground black pepper to taste

1 Assemble *mise en place* trays for this recipe (see page 6). Preheat the oven to 450 degrees F.

2 Lightly spray a heavy-duty baking sheet with nonstick vegetable spray. On the pan, toss together the potatoes, oil, and salt and pepper to taste. Spread the potatoes out into a single layer and roast, turning once, for about 15 to 20 minutes, or until tender and golden. Serve immediately.

(See page 50 for photograph)

PATRICK CLARK
Couscous and Sautéed Savoy Cabbage

SERVES 6
PREPARATION TIME: ABOUT 20 MINUTES
COOKING TIME: ABOUT 5 MINUTES

FAT PER SERVING: 5.5 GRAMS
SATURATED FAT: 2.2 GRAMS
CALORIES PER SERVING: 195
CALORIES FROM FAT: 25%

PATRICK CLARK: Couscous and Sautéed Savoy Cabbage

This easy-to-make combination is the perfect accompaniment for grilled fish or meat. To lower the saturated fat, sauté the cabbage in vegetable oil instead of butter.

3 cups water or Chicken Broth (see page 14)
½ cup finely diced carrots
1/2 cup finely diced zucchini
1/2 cup finely diced onions
1 cup quick-cooking couscous
1 tablespoon olive oil (optional)
Salt and freshly ground black pepper to taste
11/2 tablespoons unsalted butter or vegetable oil
1 head savoy cabbage, shredded, blanched, and patted dry

1 Assemble *mise en place* trays for this recipe (see page 6).

2 In a large saucepan, bring the water to a boil over high heat and add the carrots, zucchini, and onions. Stir in the couscous, cover, remove from the heat, and set aside for about 10 minutes, or until all the liquid is absorbed. Add the oil, if using, and salt and pepper to taste and fluff with a fork. Cover to keep warm.

3 In a large sauté pan, heat the butter over medium-low heat. Add the cabbage and sauté for about 3 minutes, or until just warmed through. Season to taste with salt and pepper.

4 Spoon the couscous onto one half of a large warm serving platter, mound the cabbage next to it, and serve immediately.

NANCY SILVERTON AND MARK PEEL
Potato Shoes

SERVES 6
PREPARATION TIME: ABOUT 10 MINUTES
COOKING TIME: ABOUT 30 MINUTES

FAT PER SERVING: 9.2 GRAMS
SATURATED FAT: 0.9 GRAM
CALORIES PER SERVING: 264
CALORIES FROM FAT: 31%

Nancy and Mark call these "shoes" because they truly resemble the soles of shoes for very tiny feet! If you like potatoes, you will love these.

5 small baking potatoes (4 to 6 ounces each)
1/4 cup vegetable oil
Coarse salt and freshly ground black pepper to taste

1 Assemble *mise en place* trays for this recipe (see page 6). Preheat the oven to 450 degrees F.

2 Cut the potatoes lengthwise into 1/2-inch-thick slices. (Do not peel.)

3 In an oven-proof skillet large enough to hold the potatoes in a single layer, heat the oil over medium heat and cook the potatoes for about 5 minutes, or until the bottoms are well browned. (You may need to use 2 skillets.)

4 Sprinkle the potatoes with coarse salt and pepper to taste and bake, without turning, for about 20 minutes, or until tender. Serve immediately, bottom side up.

(See page 59 for photograph)

▶ A cast-iron skillet is best for this recipe, although any oven-proof skillet works well.

▶ You can also cut and brown the potatoes in this fashion and then place under any roast (a leg of lamb is particularly good) to roast, without turning, in the fat and juices of the meat. However, this increases the fat and calorie content of the potatoes.

NANCY SILVERTON AND MARK PEEL
Roasted Onions with Mustard Vinaigrette

SERVES 6
PREPARATION TIME: ABOUT 15 MINUTES
ROASTING TIME: ABOUT 1 HOUR AND 30 MINUTES
STANDING TIME: ABOUT 15 MINUTES

FAT PER SERVING: 9 GRAMS
SATURATED FAT: 1.2 GRAMS
CALORIES PER SERVING: 128
CALORIES FROM FAT: 63%

Nancy and Mark taught us their favorite method for preparing "always-on-hand" onions. It's so easy, and absolutely perfect for dressing up simply grilled meats, poultry, or fish. To save on fat, serve the onions without the vinaigrette. Note that the percentage of calories from fat is high, but the calories and grams of saturated fat are low, making this better for you than you may at first think!

3 very large red onions, dry papery outer skin removed and halved through the stem end
2 tablespoons olive oil
1 teaspoon coarse salt
3 tablespoons fresh lemon juice
1 1/2 teaspoons chopped fresh thyme or 3/8 teaspoon dried
1 1/2 teaspoons Dijon mustard
1/4 teaspoon coarsely ground black pepper
2 tablespoons extra-virgin olive oil

1 Assemble *mise en place* trays for this recipe (see page 6). Preheat the oven to 375 degrees F.

2 In a shallow baking pan just large enough to hold them comfortably, arrange the onions cut side down in a single layer. Drizzle with the 2 tablespoons olive oil and sprinkle with the coarse salt. Roast, basting occasionally with any accumulated juices, for 1 1/2 hours, until the onions are very soft in the center, lightly browned and somewhat

NANCY SILVERTON AND MARK PEEL: Roasted Onions with Mustard Vinaigrette

caramelized, and just beginning to come apart.

3 In a small bowl, whisk together the lemon juice, thyme, mustard, and pepper. Gradually whisk in the extra-virgin olive oil. (The mixture will not emulsify.) Pour over the warm onions and set aside for about 15 minutes before serving.

▶ To roast small white onions, slice a small piece off the stem end of each so that they can stand upright in the pan. Cut an X about 1/2 inch deep into the top of each onion. Proceed with the recipe, baking the onions for about 35 to 40 minutes, until very soft. The baking time will depend on their size.

Entrées

POULTRY

Grilled Honey-Basil Chicken

Jamaican Jerk Chicken with Banana-Guava Ketchup

*Herb-Marinated Chicken, Shiitake Mushrooms,
and Roasted Potatoes Vinaigrette on Salad Greens*

Roasted Turkey Breast with Port and Dried Cranberry Sauce

MEAT

Braised Beef with Bean, Zucchini, and Pepper Salad

London Broil with Lime-Marinated Red Onions and Pineapple Ketchup

Patria Pork over Boniato Purée with Black Bean Broth

Cool Lamb Salad with Flageolets, Cumin, and Roasted Peppers

The Best Leg of Lamb with Baba Ghanoosh

FISH AND SEAFOOD

Roasted Salmon with Moroccan Barbecue Sauce

Spice-Rubbed Swordfish with Mango-Lime Salsa

*Striped Bass with Mango-Black Bean Salsa,
Chayote Squash, and Mango Sauce*

*Grilled Swordfish and Fennel with Charred Tomatoes,
Oil-Roasted Garlic, and Balsamic Vinegar*

Sole with Tomato Fondue and Saffron Pasta

Broiled Pompano with Pickles and Vegetables

Big Easy Seafood-Okra Gumbo

PASTA

Fusilli with Twenty-Minute Tomato Sauce, Hot Chiles, and Arugula

Bow Tie Pasta with Mussels and Zucchini

Ziti with Lentils and Kale

Orecchiette with Zucchini and Yellow Squash

◁◁ *(Overleaf)* GEORGES PERRIER: Sole with Tomato Fondue and Saffron Pasta

RON HOOK
Grilled Honey-Basil Chicken

SERVES 6
PREPARATION TIME: ABOUT 10 MINUTES
MARINATING TIME: AT LEAST 1 HOUR
COOKING TIME: ABOUT 7 MINUTES

FAT PER SERVING: 4.7 GRAMS
SATURATED FAT: 0.8 GRAM
CALORIES PER SERVING: 243
CALORIES FROM FAT: 18%

Here's a tasty addition to summer's grill routine. However, you can also prepare this chicken under the broiler when the weather turns cool.

1¹/₂ pounds boneless, skinless chicken breasts, split and pounded to an even thickness
1¹/₂ cups raspberry vinegar
¹/₄ cup reduced-sodium soy sauce
¹/₄ cup plus 2 tablespoons Dijon mustard
¹/₄ cup honey
¹/₄ cup plus 2 tablespoons chopped fresh basil
1 teaspoon dried thyme
1 teaspoon freshly ground black pepper

1 Assemble *mise en place* trays for this recipe (see page 6).

2 Place the chicken in a shallow glass dish. In a small mixing bowl, combine the vinegar, soy sauce, mustard, honey, basil, thyme, and pepper. Whisk well and pour over the chicken. Cover and refrigerate for at least 1 hour or up to 4 hours, turning occasionally.

3 Prepare a charcoal or gas grill or preheat the broiler. Spray the grilling grid or broiling pan with nonstick vegetable spray.

4 When the coals are very hot, lift the chicken from the marinade and grill or broil for about 3¹/₂ minutes on each side, or until just cooked through. Do not overcook.

5 Meanwhile, transfer the marinade to a small saucepan. Bring to a boil over high heat and boil for about 5 minutes, or until reduced by half.

6 Pour the reduced marinade over the chicken and serve immediately.

RON HOOK: Grilled Honey-Basil Chicken *and* Appaloosa, Butterscotch, and Chestnut Bean Salad (recipe on page 37)

Jamaican Jerk Chicken with Banana-Guava Ketchup

SERVES 6
PREPARATION TIME: ABOUT 20 MINUTES
CHILLING TIME: AT LEAST 2 HOURS
COOKING TIME: ABOUT 1 HOUR

FAT PER SERVING: 8.6 GRAMS
SATURATED FAT: 2.2 GRAMS
CALORIES PER SERVING: 199
CALORIES FROM FAT: 40%

Chicken thighs and legs are used in this recipe because their center bones allow them to withstand long, slow grilling and still remain juicy. You could, of course, substitute skinned chicken breasts, which are slightly lower in fat, but take extra care that they do not dry out. A jerk is a thick paste used for seasoning.

10 Scotch Bonnet or other very hot chiles, stemmed
3 scallions, finely chopped
1/4 cup yellow mustard
Juice of 2 limes
2 tablespoons fresh orange juice
2 tablespoons white vinegar, plus more if necessary
2 tablespoons dried rosemary
2 tablespoons dried basil
2 tablespoons dried thyme
2 tablespoons chopped fresh flat-leaf parsley
2 tablespoons mustard seeds
1 teaspoon salt
1 teaspoon freshly ground black pepper
6 chicken leg-thigh quarters (thighs with legs attached), skin removed
Banana-Guava Ketchup (recipe follows)

1 Assemble *mise en place* trays for this recipe (see page 6).

2 In a blender, combine the chiles, scallions, mustard, lime and orange juices, vinegar, herbs, mustard seeds, salt, and pepper and process to a thick paste. If the paste seems too thick, thin with a little more vinegar. Transfer to a nonreactive container, cover, and refrigerate for at least 2 hours.

3 Prepare a charcoal or gas grill.

4 Generously rub the chicken with the seasoning paste. Grill, uncovered, over a very low fire for about 1 hour, or until the meat easily pulls away from the bone. (If the heat is properly low, the chicken will not burn or dry out.)

5 Separate the legs from the thighs by cutting through the joint. Serve hot or at room temperature with the Banana-Guava Ketchup.

NOTE: You can also roast this chicken in a 275- or 300-degree-F oven for about 1 1/2 hours, or until the meat easily pulls away from the bone.

The jerk paste will keep, refrigerated, almost indefinitely. Double the amount so that you will have it on hand to add zest to other grilled poultry or meat.

▶ **You can replace the chiles with 1/4 cup Inner Beauty or other Caribbean-style hot sauce, or a mixture of chiles of varying degrees of heat (you will probably need about 15 chiles to approximate the heat of the Scotch Bonnets).**

▶ **You can leave the skin on for juicier chicken, but the fat grams will increase accordingly.**

BANANA-GUAVA KETCHUP

MAKES ABOUT 2 CUPS
FAT PER 5-TABLESPOON SERVING: 3 GRAMS
SATURATED FAT: 0.4 GRAM
CALORIES PER SERVING: 186
CALORIES FROM FAT: 14%

1 tablespoon vegetable oil
1 medium yellow onion (about 4 ounces), diced
5 very ripe bananas (about 2 pounds), peeled and cut into 1-inch pieces
1/2 cup guava paste
1 1/2 cups fresh orange juice
2 1/2 tablespoons raisins
2 tablespoons light brown sugar
1 tablespoon curry powder
2 tablespoons white vinegar
1/4 cup fresh lime juice (about 2 limes)
Salt and cracked black pepper to taste

1 In a heavy-bottomed saucepan, heat the oil over medium heat. Add the onions and sauté for about 5 minutes, or until very soft. Reduce the heat slightly, add the bananas, and cook, stirring constantly to avoid sticking, for about 5 minutes, or until the bananas are slightly caramelized.

2 Combine the guava paste with 1 cup of the orange juice

CHRIS SCHELESINGER: Jamaican Jerk Chicken with Banana-Guava Ketchup ▷

and stir into the banana mixture. Add the raisins, brown sugar, curry powder, 1 tablespoon of the vinegar, and the remaining 1/2 cup orange juice and stir to combine. Raise the heat and bring to a boil. Reduce the heat and simmer gently for about 15 minutes, or until the mixture is the consistency of applesauce.

3 Remove from the heat and stir in the lime juice and the remaining 1 tablespoon vinegar. Season with salt and cracked pepper to taste. Serve hot or at room temperature.

NOTE: The guava paste combined with 1 cup orange juice can be replaced by one 12-ounce can guava nectar or 1 cup guava jelly combined with 1/2 cup orange juice.

▶ **Banana-Guava Ketchup will keep, covered, and refrigerated, for up to 6 weeks. (It will firm up considerably as it cools.) It is a tasty condiment for grilled meats, as well as in sandwiches.**

MARIE SIMMONS
Herb-Marinated Chicken, Shiitake Mushrooms, and Roasted Potatoes Vinaigrette on Salad Greens

SERVES 6
PREPARATION TIME: ABOUT 45 MINUTES
MARINATING TIME: AT LEAST 30
   MINUTES
COOKING TIME: ABOUT 35 MINUTES

FAT PER SERVING: 17 GRAMS
SATURATED FAT: 3 GRAMS
CALORIES PER SERVING: 592
CALORIES FROM FAT: 27%

Marie calls this a "salad supper," since all the elements are combined on one plate over salad greens. It is a pristine example of contemporary health-conscious fare.

3 cloves garlic, minced
1 tablespoon grated orange or lemon zest
1 1/2 tablespoons plus 1/2 teaspoon fresh thyme leaves
1/2 teaspoon salt, plus more to taste
1/4 teaspoon coarsely ground black pepper, plus more to taste
3 boneless, skinless chicken breasts, split and pounded thin, or 1 1/2 pounds chicken tenders
6 medium baking potatoes, cut into 1/4-inch-thick slices
1/4 cup plus 1 tablespoon extra-virgin olive oil
3 tablespoons fruit-flavored red wine vinegar, such as raspberry
6 large shiitake mushroom caps
2 small red bell peppers, cored, seeded, and sliced into thin strips
1/4 cup chopped fresh flat-leaf parsley
9 cups mixed salad greens, such as Boston, bibb, red leaf, arugula, watercress, and/or mâche

1 Assemble *mise en place* trays for this recipe (see page 6).

2 On a flat plate, combine the garlic, zest, the 1 1/2 tablespoons thyme, 1/2 teaspoon salt, and 1/4 teaspoon pepper. Lay the chicken pieces on the plate and gently rub the mix

MARIE SIMMONS: Herb-Marinated Chicken, Shiitake Mushrooms, and Roasted Potatoes Vinaigrette on Salad Greens

ture into them. Cover and refrigerate for at least 30 minutes.

3 Preheat the oven to 400 degrees F.

4 Put the potatoes in a bowl. Drizzle with 2 tablespoons of the oil, sprinkle with salt and pepper to taste, and toss to coat. Arrange on a nonstick baking sheet and bake for about 20 minutes, or until golden and crisp on the bottom. Carefully turn and bake for 15 minutes longer, or until tender. Cover and set aside to keep warm.

5 Meanwhile, make the vinaigrette. In a small bowl, whisk together 2 tablespoons of the oil, the vinegar, the remaining 1/2 teaspoon thyme, and salt and pepper to taste. Set aside.

6 While the potatoes are baking, heat a large nonstick skillet over medium heat until hot enough to evaporate a drop of water on contact. Add 2 teapoons of the oil and tilt the pan to coat. Add the chicken and cook for about 1 minute per side, or until nicely browned and cooked through. (If the chicken pieces are thicker than 1/4 inch, you may need to cook them for up to 3 minutes per side.) Transfer the chicken to a warm plate and cover to keep warm.

7 Add the remaining 1 teaspoon oil to the pan. Add the mushrooms and bell peppers and cook for 2 minutes. Sprinkle with salt to taste, stir gently, and cook for about 2 more minutes, or until just barely tender. Transfer to the plate with the chicken and sprinkle with the parsley.

8 Put the salad greens in a large bowl and toss with half of the vinaigrette. Place equal portions on each plate. If using whole chicken breasts, cut into thin diagonal slices, and arrange the slices or tenders on top of the greens. Cut the mushroom caps into 1/4-inch strips and arrange them and the bell pepper strips on top of the chicken. Sprinkle the hot potatoes with the remaining vinaigrette and arrange them around the salads. Serve immediately.

▶ **Almost any vegetable works in this salad. Marie particularly recommends steamed green beans, broccoli florets, or sugar snap peas. Sautéed cherry tomatoes also make a pretty—and tasty—addition.**

PATRICIA JAMIESON

Roasted Turkey Breast with Port and Dried Cranberry Sauce

SERVES 6
PREPARATION TIME: ABOUT 1 HOUR
MARINATING TIME: AT LEAST 1 HOUR OR
   UP TO 8 HOURS
COOKING TIME: ABOUT 1 HOUR AND 15
   MINUTES

FAT PER SERVING: 6.5 GRAMS
SATURATED FAT: 1.3 GRAMS
CALORIES PER SERVING: 225
CALORIES FROM FAT: 26%

A low-calorie holiday bird with no leftovers! If you bone the turkey breast yourself, by all means make a dark turkey stock with the bones. Roast them first and then proceed as for Chicken Stock (see page 14).

2 tablespoons Dijon mustard
1 tablespoon plus 1 teaspoon orange juice concentrate, thawed
One 1 1/2-pound boneless turkey breast, skin left on
Freshly ground black pepper to taste
2/3 cup dried cranberries
1/2 cup water
1 tablespoon vegetable oil
2 onions, chopped
1 cup plus 1 tablespoon port wine

3 tablespoons balsamic vinegar
2 cups Chicken Stock (see page 14)
6 sprigs fresh thyme
1/2 teaspoon crushed black peppercorns
Two to three 1/2-inch-wide strips orange zest
2 1/2 teaspoons arrowroot

1 Assemble *mise en place* trays for this recipe (see page 6).

2 In a small bowl, combine the mustard and orange juice concentrate. Set aside.

3 Starting at the tip of the turkey breast, peel back the skin, leaving it attached at the wishbone end. Trim any fat and membrane from the turkey. Put the turkey in a shallow glass dish and rub the meat all over with the mustard mixture. Season generously with pepper. Stretch the skin back over the flesh and secure with toothpicks so that it covers the top of the breast well. Cover and refrigerate for at least 1 hour, or up to 8 hours.

PATRICIA JAMIESON:
Roasted Turkey Breast
with Port and Dried
Cranberry Sauce; Wild
Rice–Orzo Pilaf *and*
Roasted Sweet Potatoes
(see page 39 for side dish
recipes).

4 In a small saucepan, combine the cranberries and water and bring to a boil over medium heat. Reduce the heat and simmer for 3 minutes. Drain, reserving the cooking water. Set the cranberries and cooking liquid aside separately.

5 In a medium-sized saucepan, heat 2 teaspoons of the oil over medium-low heat. Add half the onions and cook, stirring occasionally, for about 10 minutes, or until tender and golden. Add 1 cup of the port and the vinegar, raise the heat to high, and bring to a boil. Boil for about 5 minutes, or until reduced by half. Add the stock, the reserved cranberry water, 2 thyme sprigs, and the crushed peppercorns. Return to a boil and boil for 10 minutes, or until reduced by half. Set aside.

6 Preheat the oven to 325 degrees F. Lightly oil a small roasting pan or an oven-proof skillet that can accommodate a rack.

7 Place the remaining onions and 4 thyme sprigs and the orange zest in the center of the prepared pan and set a rack over them. Lightly spray the rack with vegetable oil spray. Set the turkey breast on the rack and roast for about 45 minutes, or until a meat thermometer inserted in the thick-

est part registers 160 to 165 degrees F and the juices run clear when the turkey is pierced in the thickest part. Transfer the turkey to a carving board, cover loosely, and let rest for 10 to 20 minutes. (The internal temperature will increase to 170 degrees F upon resting.)

8 Remove the rack from the roasting pan and place the pan over medium heat. Pour in the port reduction and bring to a boil, stirring to scrape up any brown bits. Strain through a fine sieve into a small saucepan, pressing down on the onions.

9 Place the pan over medium heat and bring to a simmer. In a small bowl, dissolve the arrowroot in the remaining 1 tablespoon port, and add to the sauce. Cook, stirring constantly, for about 3 minutes, or until the sauce thickens slightly and is glossy. Stir in the cranberries and adjust the seasoning with pepper.

10 Remove the toothpicks and discard the turkey skin. Holding the knife more or less parallel to the cutting board, slice the turkey. Arrange the slices on a platter or individual plates, spoon a little sauce over the meat, and pass the rest on the side.

NOTE: The port reduction and the plumped cranberries can be prepared up to 8 hours ahead. Store separately, covered and refrigerated. The recipe can be doubled. If you do so, allow extra time for the sauce to reduce.

▶ As with all recipes in the book, if using canned broth in place of homemade stock, use reduced-sodium broth.

▶ The turkey skin serves as a blanket to prevent the turkey from drying out as it roasts, but it is removed before serving to cut the fat.

JEAN-MICHEL BERGOUGNOUX

Braised Beef with Bean, Zucchini, and Pepper Salad

SERVES 6
PREPARATION TIME: ABOUT 1 HOUR
COOKING TIME: ABOUT 2 HOURS AND 35
    MINUTES
FAT PER SERVING: 20 GRAMS
SATURATED FAT: 6 GRAMS
CALORIES PER SERVING: 853
CALORIES FROM FAT: 22%

This wonderful braised beef incorporates all of the flavors and many of the colors of Provence. It is delicious served at room temperature, too.

1 tablespoon olive oil
4 pounds beef chuck or top round roast, well trimmed
2 carrots, peeled and finely diced
1 large onion, finely diced
2 ribs celery, finely diced
2 medium-sized tomatoes, cored and quartered
1 head garlic, cut in half crosswise
1 long strip orange zest
1 bunch fresh flat-leaf parsley
4 sprigs fresh thyme
1 bay leaf
1 teaspoon black peppercorns
6 cups dry white wine
Sauce Hachée (recipe follows)
Bean, Zucchini, and Pepper Salad (recipe follows)

■ Special Equipment: Large heavy-bottomed oven-proof skillet with lid

1 Assemble *mise en place* trays for this recipe (see page 6). Preheat the oven to 350 degrees F.

2 In a large heavy-bottomed oven-proof skillet, heat the oil over medium heat. Add the beef and brown well on all sides, about 5 minutes. Transfer to a plate.

3 Add the carrots, onions, and celery to the skillet and sauté 3 minutes, or until tender.

4 Return the beef to the skillet, add the tomatoes, garlic, orange zest, parsley, thyme, bay leaf, peppercorns, and wine and bring to a boil. Cover, transfer to the oven, and bake for 2½ hours, or until the beef is very tender but still firm to the touch. Do not allow the liquid to boil—it should barely simmer as the meat braises; reduce the oven temperature if necessary.

5 Lift the beef from the skillet and cut it into 6 slices. Place a slice on each plate and spoon 2 tablespoons sauce over it. Mound the salad next to the meat.

SAUCE HACHÉE

MAKES ABOUT 1 CUP
FAT PER 2-TABLESPOON SERVING: 13.6 GRAMS
SATURATED FAT: 1.8 GRAMS
CALORIES PER SERVING: 128
CALORIES FROM FAT: 93%

¼ cup dry white wine
1½ teaspoons balsamic vinegar
½ teaspoon Dijon mustard
½ cup olive oil
1 anchovy fillet, drained well and chopped
3 tablespoons peeled, seeded, and diced tomatoes
1 teaspoon chopped Niçoise olives
½ teaspoon chopped capers
½ teaspoon chopped cornichons
1 tablespoon chopped fresh flat-leaf parsley
1½ teaspoons chopped fresh basil
Salt and freshly ground black pepper to taste

In a small bowl, whisk together the wine, vinegar, and mustard. Whisk in the oil until emulsified. Fold in the anchovy, tomatoes, olives, capers, cornichons, herbs, and salt and pepper to taste. Serve immediately.

NOTE: The sauce can be made up to 1 day ahead, but do not add the herbs until just before serving.

BEAN, ZUCCHINI, AND PEPPER SALAD

SERVES 6
FAT PER SERVING: 5.2 GRAMS
SATURATED FAT: 0.7 GRAM
CALORIES PER SERVING: 109
CALORIES FROM FAT: 40%

1 pound zucchini, julienned (avoid the seedy centers)
1½ pounds yellow wax beans, trimmed
1 rcd bell pepper
2 bunches fresh basil, leaves only
Coarse salt to taste
2 tablespoons olive oil
Freshly ground black pepper to taste

■ Special Equipment: Mortar and pestle

1 Blanch the zucchini in boiling salted water for 1 minute. Drain and refresh under cold running water. Pat dry and set aside.

2 Blanch the beans in boiling lightly salted water for 1 minute. Drain and refresh under cold running water. Drain and set aside.

3 Using a vegetable peeler, remove the thin outer skin from the bell pepper. Cut the pepper in half and remove the core, membrane, and seeds. Cut into a fine julienne.

4 Put the basil leaves in a large mortar and add coarse salt to taste. Pulverize, using the pestle, while slowly adding the oil to make a thick paste.

5 In a large bowl, combine the zucchini, beans, and bell pepper. Add the basil paste and toss to coat. Season to taste with additional salt if necessary and pepper.

NOTE: The vegetables and the basil paste can be prepared up to 1 day ahead. Store, covered and refrigerated, and combine just before serving. If wax beans are unavailable, you can replace them with green beans, but the salad will not be as colorful.

You can make the basil paste in a mini food processor, but it will not have the same texture as that made using a mortar and pestle.

CHRIS SCHLESINGER

London Broil with Lime-Marinated Red Onions and Pineapple Ketchup

SERVES 6
PREPARATION TIME: ABOUT 15 MINUTES
MARINATING TIME (ONIONS ONLY): AT
  LEAST 2 HOURS
COOKING TIME: ABOUT 20 MINUTES

FAT PER SERVING: 10.2 GRAMS
SATURATED FAT: 3.5 GRAMS
CALORIES PER SERVING: 288
CALORIES FROM FAT: 33%

Onions marinated as they are here would highlight any grilled meat or poultry just as deliciously as they do this stove-top London broil. They could also serve as a fat-free garnish on a sandwich or burger.

3 red onions, very thinly sliced
¼ cup plus 2 tablespoon fresh lime juice (about 3 limes)
Tabasco sauce to taste
2 tablespoons coarse salt
¼ cup coarsely cracked black pepper
1½ pounds London broil (top round), about 1 inch thick

◁ JEAN-MICHEL BERGOUGNOUX: Braised Beef with Bean, Zucchini, and Pepper Salad

¼ cup plus 2 tablespoons all-purpose flour
Pineapple Ketchup (recipe follows)

1 Assemble *mise en place* trays for this recipe (see page 6).

2 In a nonreactive container, combine the onions, lime juice, and Tabasco. Cover and refrigerate, tossing occasionally, for at least 2 hours or up to 8 hours.

3 Rub the coarse salt and pepper into the meat and sprinkle 3 tablespoons flour over each side. Heat a dry large heavy nonstick skillet over high heat. Add the meat and sear for about 7 minutes per side for rare. Slice on the diagonal into ¼-inch-thick slices. Serve immediately, garnished with the marinated onions and Pineapple Ketchup.

▶ **For meat that is more well done, sear until it is almost the degree of doneness you prefer. Remove the meat from pan and allow to rest for 2 minutes before cutting. The resting time allows the meat to finish cooking.**

PINEAPPLE KETCHUP

MAKES ABOUT 2¹/₂ CUPS
FAT PER SERVING: 5 GRAMS
SATURATED FAT: 0.9 GRAM
CALORIES PER SERVING: 135
CALORIES FROM FAT: 32%

1 tablespoon vegetable oil
1 yellow onion, very thinly sliced
¹/₂ large ripe pineapple, peeled, cored, and cut into ¹/₂-inch
cubes (about 1¹/₂ cups)
¹/₄ cup fresh orange juice
¹/₄ cup tamarind water (see Note)
¹/₄ cup packed light brown sugar
Pinch of ground cloves
Salt and coarsely cracked black pepper to taste

1 In a heavy-bottomed sauté pan, heat the oil over high
heat until very hot but not smoking. Add the onions,
reduce the heat, and sauté for about 7 minutes, or until
translucent.

2 Add the pineapple and cook, stirring constantly, for
about 3 minutes, or until the pineapple begins to soften.

3 Add the orange juice, tamarind water, sugar, cloves, and
salt and cracked pepper to taste. Cook, stirring constantly,
for about 5 minutes, or until heated through. Remove from
the heat and serve hot or at room temperature. This
ketchup keeps, covered and refrigerated, for up to 2 weeks.

NOTE: To make tamarind water, combine 1 tablespoon
tamarind syrup with ¹/₂ cup hot water. Or dissolve a golf
ball-sized piece of tamarind paste in ¹/₂ cup very hot water
and allow to sit for 10 minutes; strain through a fine sieve
to remove all the pulp. Chris also told us that equal parts of
molasses, fresh lime juice, and Worcestershire sauce will be
a valiant approximation for the natural flavor of tamarind.
If necessary, you can substitute ¹/₄ cup white vinegar for the
tamarind water.

CHRIS SCHLESINGER: London Broil with Lime-Marinated Red Onions
and Pineapple Ketchup

DOUGLAS RODRIGUEZ
Patria Pork over Boniato Purée with Black Bean Broth

SERVES 6
PREPARATION TIME: ABOUT 1 HOUR
MARINATING TIME: AT LEAST 12 HOURS
COOKING TIME: ABOUT 2 HOURS AND 40
   MINUTES

FAT PER SERVING: 17 GRAMS
SATURATED FAT: 5 GRAMS
CALORIES PER SERVING: 517
CALORIES FROM FAT: 32%

The flavors, colors, and texture of this dish perfectly illustrate Doug's cooking, which is zesty, slightly off-beat, and very delicious. Doug uses the more traditional Latin boneless pork butt for this recipe, but we chose pork tenderloin to create a lighter version.

2¹/₂ pounds pork tenderloin, trimmed of all fat
¹/₄ cup white vinegar
3 bay leaves
¹/₂ cup chopped white onions
³/₄ cup chopped fresh cilantro
2 tablespoons fresh thyme leaves
2 tablespoons fresh oregano leaves
8 cloves garlic
1 tablespoon cumin seeds
2 tablespoons coarse salt
Freshly ground black pepper to taste
3 cups water
2 tablespoons olive oil
8 cachucha chiles or other hot green chiles, or to taste, seeded and finely diced
¹/₂ cup fresh lime juice (about 4 limes)
Black Bean Broth (recipe follows)
Boniato Purée (recipe follows)

1 Assemble *mise en place* trays for this recipe (see page 6).

2 Put the pork in a nonreactive baking pan large enough to hold it comfortably. In a blender, combine the vinegar, bay leaves, onions, ¹/₄ cup of the cilantro, the thyme, oregano, garlic, cumin, coarse salt, and pepper to taste. With the motor running, slowly add the water and blend to a purée. Pour over the pork, cover, and refrigerate for at least 12 hours, turning occasionally.

3 Preheat the oven to 300 degrees F.

4 Put the pan holding the pork and marinade into the oven and roast, covered, for about 2¹/₂ hours, or until the pork is very well done and almost falling apart. Cool in the liquid

for about 1 hour. Lift the pork from the pan and, using 2 forks, pull apart into shreds.

5 In a large heavy sauté pan, heat the oil over medium-high heat. Add the shredded pork, chiles, and the remaining ¹/₂ cup chopped cilantro and sauté for about 10 minutes, or until the meat is crispy. Add the lime juice, toss, and remove from the heat.

6 Place a scoop of Boniato Purée in the center of each plate, arrange some pork on top, and ladle the Black Bean Broth all around. Serve immediately.

DOUGLAS RODRIGUEZ: Patria Pork over Boniato Purée with Black Bean Broth

Black Bean Broth

MAKES ABOUT 2 CUPS
FAT PER 2 1/2-TABLESPOON SERVING: 0.3 GRAM
SATURATED FAT: 0
CALORIES PER SERVING: 62.5
CALORIES FROM FAT: 4%

1 pound dried black beans, rinsed and picked clean
2 bay leaves
1 teaspoon ground cumin
1 teaspoon chopped fresh oregano
8 cups cold water
6 red bell peppers, cored, seeded, and quartered
2 white onions, quartered
20 cloves garlic

■ Special Equipment: Juice extractor

1 In a large saucepan, combine the beans, bay leaves, cumin, oregano, and water and bring to a boil over high heat. Reduce the heat and simmer for about 2 hours, or until the beans soften.

2 Process the bell peppers, onions, and garlic in a juice extractor and add the extracted juice to the beans, discarding the pulp. Cook the beans for an additional 30 minutes, or until tender.

3 Strain the cooking liquid through a fine sieve into a saucepan. (Reserve the beans for another use.) Bring the liquid to a boil over high heat, reduce the heat, and simmer for about 20 minutes, or until reduced to 2 cups. Serve hot.

Boniato Purée

MAKES ABOUT 6 CUPS
FAT PER 1-CUP SERVING: 0.6 GRAM
SATURATED FAT: 0.2 GRAM
CALORIES PER SERVING: 176
CALORIES FROM FAT: 3%

1 1/2 pounds boniato, peeled and diced
4 cups skim milk
2 cups water
Salt to taste

1 In a large saucepan, combine the boniato, milk, and water and bring to a boil over high heat. Reduce the heat and simmer for about 1 hour, or until the boniato is very tender when pierced with a fork. Drain, reserving the cooking liquid.

2 Using a potato masher, mash the boniato, adding just enough of the reserved liquid to keep it moist. Season to taste with salt and serve hot.

NOTE: The purée can be made up to 2 days ahead, covered, and refrigerated. Reheat in a microwave or in the top half of a double boiler over boiling water.

▶ **Boniato, also called Cuban sweet potato, is sold in Latin and Asian markets.**

MARIO BATALI

Cool Lamb Salad with Flageolet, Cumin, and Roasted Peppers

SERVES 6
PREPARATION TIME: ABOUT 1 HOUR
MARINATING TIME: AT LEAST 12 HOURS
COOKING TIME: ABOUT 1 HOUR
FAT PER SERVING: 17 GRAMS
SATURATED FAT: 4 GRAMS
CALORIES PER SERVING: 340
CALORIES FROM FAT: 47%

A bit of Provence, a bit of the Middle East, and a taste of Italy absolutely define Mario Batali's approach to contemporary cooking in this spectacular main-coarse salad. To cut back on calories and fat, reduce the amount of lamb.

One 1 1/2-pound boneless leg of lamb, butterflied
3 tablespoons olive oil
2 cups plain nonfat yogurt
1 bunch fresh rosemary, leaves only
1 bunch fresh mint
6 cloves garlic
1/4 cup black peppercorns
1 large head frisée
1 tablespoon extra-virgin olive oil
1 teaspoon fresh lemon juice
Coarse salt and freshly ground black pepper to taste
Marinated Flageolets (recipe follows)
Roasted Peppers (recipe follows)
Cumin-Scented Yogurt (recipe follows)

1 Assemble *mise en place* trays for this recipe (see page 6).

2 Put the lamb in a shallow nonreactive dish. In a food processor fitted with the metal blade, combine the yogurt, olive oil, yogurt, rosemary, mint, garlic, and peppercorns, and using quick on and off pulses, process just until the herbs and garlic are chopped. Do not purée. Pour over the lamb, cover, and refrigerate for at least 12 hours.

3 Prepare a charcoal or gas grill or preheat the broiler.

4 Grill the lamb for about 12 minutes on each side for medium rare. Place on a warm platter and let rest for about 10 minutes. If broiling, broil the lamb about 4 inches from the heat source.

5 Toss the frisée with the extra-virgin olive oil, lemon juice, and coarse salt and pepper to taste. Place equal portions on each plate and top with the flageolets and roasted peppers. Slice the lamb on the diagonal into 1/4-inch-thick slices and arrange over the salads. Spoon the yogurt over the top and around the salad. Serve immediately.

NOTE: Mario suggests using Coach Farm whole goats' milk yogurt in the recipes, but, in the interest of reducing fat, we chose readily available nonfat cows' milk yogurt.

MARINATED FLAGEOLETS

MAKES ABOUT 2 CUPS
FAT PER 1/3-CUP SERVING: 6.9 GRAMS
SATURATED FAT: 1 GRAM
CALORIES PER SERVING: 117
CALORIES FROM FAT: 53%

1 cup dried flageolets or small white beans, rinsed and picked clean
1/4 cup red wine vinegar
3 tablespoons extra-virgin olive oil
1/4 teaspoon fresh oregano or 1/8 teaspoon dried
1/4 teaspoon cayenne pepper
1/4 large red onion, thinly sliced
Coarse salt and freshly ground black pepper to taste

1 Put the beans in a large saucepan, add 6 cups cold water, and soak for about 8 hours.

2 Drain and rinse the beans, return to the pan, and add 6 cups cold water. Bring to a boil over high heat, reduce the heat, and simmer for about 45 minutes, or until *al dente*. Drain, transfer the beans to a nonreactive bowl, and set aside to cool.

3 In a small bowl, whisk together the vinegar, oil, oregano, and cayenne. Toss in the onion and season to taste with coarse salt and pepper. Pour over the beans and set aside to marinate for at least 30 minutes. Serve at room temperature, or store, covered and refrigerated, for up to 1 day. Bring to room temperature before serving.

ROASTED PEPPERS

MAKES ABOUT 1 CUP
FAT PER 3-TABLESPOON SERVING: 0.1 GRAM
SATURATED FAT: 0.1 GRAM
CALORIES PER SERVING: 7
CALORIES FROM FAT: 6%

2 large red bell peppers, roasted, peeled, cored, and seeded (see page 12)
1 teaspoon extra-virgin olive oil
Coarse salt and freshly ground black pepper to taste

Using tiny decorative cutters or a sharp paring knife, cut the roasted peppers into triangles, stars, or other fancy shapes. Put in a small bowl and toss with the oil and coarse salt and pepper to taste. Serve at room temperature, or store, covered and refrigerated, for up to 2 days. Bring to room temperature before serving.

CUMIN-SCENTED YOGURT

MAKES ABOUT 1 CUP
FAT PER 3-TABLESPOON SERVING: 0
SATURATED FAT: 0
CALORIES PER SERVING: 21
CALORIES FROM FAT: 0%

1 cup plain nonfat yogurt
1 teaspoon fresh lemon juice
1 tablespoon toasted ground cumin (see Note)
1/4 teaspoon salt

In a blender, process the yogurt, juice, cumin, and salt for about 1 minute, or until smooth. Serve immediately or store, covered and refrigerated, for up to 1 week.

NOTE: Toast the cumin in a small skillet over low heat, stirring once or twice, for approximately 2 minutes, or just until lightly browned and aromatic.

(Overleaf) **MARIO BATALI:** Cool Lamb Salad with Flageolet, Cumin, and Roasted Peppers ▷▷

NANCY SILVERTON AND MARK PEEL
The Best Leg of Lamb with Baba Ghanoosh

SERVES 6
PREPARATION TIME: ABOUT 1 HOUR
MARINATING TIME: AT LEAST 4 HOURS
COOKING TIME: ABOUT 1 HOUR AND 10
    MINUTES

FAT PER SERVING: 30 GRAMS
SATURATED FAT: 9.7 GRAMS
CALORIES PER SERVING: 703
CALORIES FROM FAT: 39%

Nancy and Mark call for an enormous bouquet of rosemary, an herb traditionally served with lamb for good reason. Even if the rosemary didn't impart a wonderful flavor to the meat, the intoxicating aroma coming from the oven would be reason enough to use it in quantity. Have the butcher remove the small bone from the leg of lamb to make slicing it easier. Serve smaller portions of lamb to reduce calories and fat amounts.

One 4½-pound leg of lamb, trimmed of excess fat
3 large cloves garlic, thinly sliced
About 1 tablespoon olive oil
Coarse salt and freshly ground black pepper to taste
6 ounces fresh rosemary (about 8 bunches)
Baba Ghanoosh (recipe follows)

1 Assemble *mise en place* trays for this recipe (see page 6).

2 Make narrow 1-inch-deep slits all over the lamb and insert the garlic slices in them. Rub the lamb all over with olive oil and coat heavily with coarse salt and pepper. Wrap tightly in plastic wrap and refrigerate for at least 4 hours, or overnight.

3 Preheat the oven to 500 degrees F.

4 Heat an oven-proof skillet or heavy saucepan large enough to hold the lamb comfortably over high heat. Add the lamb and brown on all sides. Remove to a platter and pour off all but 1 tablespoon of fat from the pan. Cover the bottom of the pan with a bed of rosemary (using half to two thirds of the rosemary) and place the lamb on top. Cover the lamb with the rest of the rosemary.

5 Roast for 20 minutes, then reduce the oven temperature to 375 degrees F and roast for about 40 minutes longer, or until the lamb is medium-rare.

6 Take the entire pan outdoors and carefully ignite the rosemary on top of the lamb. Allow it to burn itself out;

use a tight-fitting lid to extinguish the flames if necessary. Brush off the woody stems and let the meat rest for 10 to 15 minutes.

7 Cut the lamb into thin slices. Spread the Baba Ghanoosh on a serving platter and lay the lamb slices on top. Pour any accumulated lamb juices over all and serve immediately.

NOTE: If you live in an apartment or the weather is inclement, omit flaming the rosemary. But if possible, give it a try, as the charred rosemary imparts a great flavor to the lamb.

NANCY SILVERTON AND MARK PEEL: The Best Leg of Lamb with Baba Ghanoosh and Potato Shoes (see page 40)

Baba Ghanoosh

MAKES ABOUT 2 1/2 CUPS
FAT PER 1/2-CUP SERVING: 4.5 GRAMS
SATURATED FAT: 0.6 GRAM
CALORIES PER SERVING: 51
CALORIES FROM FAT: 77%

1 large or 2 small eggplants
2 cloves garlic, minced
3 tablespoons olive oil
1 1/2 teaspoons fresh lemon juice
1/2 teaspoon coarse salt
1/2 teaspoon coarsely ground black pepper

1 Set a large cast-iron skillet over medium-high heat, add the eggplant, and cook for about 1 hour, carefully turning every 15 minutes or so, until the skin gets black and charred. Set aside until cool enough to handle.

2 Trim the stem end(s) from the eggplant and cut in half lengthwise. Carefully scrape out the pulp, discarding the charred skin. (The pulp may be darkened, which will impart a roasted flavor.)

3 Transfer the pulp to a bowl and mash it with a fork, breaking up any large pieces. Add the garlic, oil, lemon juice, coarse salt, and pepper. Cover and let stand for about 4 hours at room temperature, or refrigerate for up to 12 hours. Bring to room temperature before serving.

NOTE: You can use 2 skillets to cook the eggplant if necessary.

PATRICK CLARK

Roasted Salmon with Moroccan Barbecue Sauce

SERVES 6
PREPARATION TIME: ABOUT 15 MINUTES
COOKING TIME: ABOUT 1 HOUR

FAT PER SERVING: 25.1 GRAMS
SATURATED FAT: 5 GRAMS
CALORIES PER SERVING: 923
CALORIES FROM FAT: 24%

Patrick serves this aromatic salmon on a bed of Couscous and Sautéed Savoy Cabbage (see page 40) for a complete, light-tasting main course.

2 1/2 cups honey
1 cup ketchup
1 cup rice wine vinegar
1/2 cup soy sauce
Juice of 2 limes
1 tablespoon chile paste with garlic
1/2 cup chopped fresh cilantro
2 tablespoons chopped fresh ginger
5 star anise
2 small cinnamon sticks
1 tablespoon coriander seeds
1 tablespoon black peppercorns
1 teaspoon ground cardamom
1 teaspoon ground cloves
1 teaspoon ground mace
Six 4-ounce skinless salmon fillets
Coarse salt and freshly ground black pepper to taste
2 tablespoons cracked black pepper
2 tablespoons fennel seeds

PATRICK CLARK: Roasted Salmon with Moroccan Barbecue Sauce

1 Assemble *mise en place* trays for this recipe (see page 6).

2 In a medium-sized nonreactive saucepan, combine the honey, ketchup, vinegar, soy sauce, lime juice, chile paste, cilantro, ginger, star anise, cinnamon sticks, coriander seeds, peppercorns, cardamom, cloves, and mace and bring to a boil over medium heat. Reduce the heat and simmer, stirring frequently, for about 45 minutes, or until reduced by one third. Strain through a fine strainer into a bowl and discard the solids. Cool to room temperature.

3 Preheat the oven to 400 degrees F.

4 Season the salmon to taste with coarse salt and pepper, lay on a heavy-duty baking sheet, and bake for 7 minutes. Remove from the oven and lightly coat each side with the sauce. Sprinkle with the cracked pepper and fennel seeds and roast for an additional 3 minutes, or until the fish is opaque and just beginning to flake. Serve hot, drizzled with additional sauce.

NOTE: Chile paste with garlic is available in Asian markets and specialty food stores. The sauce can be made up to 2 weeks ahead, covered, and refrigerated. Bring to room temperature before serving.

CHRIS SCHLESINGER

Spice-Rubbed Swordfish with Mango-Lime Salsa

SERVES 6
PREPARATION TIME: ABOUT 30 MINUTES
GRILLING TIME (FISH ONLY): ABOUT 15
  MINUTES

FAT PER SERVING: 7.7 GRAMS
SATURATED FAT: 1.6 GRAMS
CALORIES PER SERVING: 220
CALORIES FROM FAT: 32%

NOTE: The spice rub can be made up to 1 month ahead, tightly covered, and kept in a cool, dark spot.

Refreshing and easy to prepare, this slightly smoky swordfish is a wonderful addition to your repertoire of low-fat summer grilling.

3 tablespoons cumin seeds
3 tablespoons chile powder
2 tablespoons coarse salt
2 tablespoons cracked black pepper
1 1/2 tablespoons curry powder
1 1/2 tablespoons ground cinnamon
Six 4-ounce swordfish steaks, about 3/4 inch thick
Mango-Lime Salsa (recipe follows)

1 Assemble *mise en place* trays for this recipe (see page 6).

2 In a heavy sauté pan, combine the cumin, chile powder, coarse salt, pepper, curry powder, and cinnamon and toast over medium heat, stirring frequently, for about 4 minutes, or until slightly smoky. Set aside to cool.

3 Prepare a charcoal or gas grill or preheat a broiler.

4 Rub the fish on both sides with the cooled spice mixture. Grill over medium-hot coals for about 7 minutes on each side, or until opaque throughout. If broiling, broil the fish 5 to 6 inches from the heat source. Serve with the Mango-Lime Salsa on the side.

MANGO-LIME SALSA

MAKES ABOUT 3 CUPS
FAT PER 1/2-CUP SERVING: 0.4 GRAM
SATURATED FAT: 0.1 GRAM
CALORIES PER SERVING: 82
CALORIES FROM FAT: 4%

2 large ripe but firm mangoes, peeled, pitted, and cut into 1/4-inch dice
1 red onion, cut into 1/4-inch dice
1 red bell pepper, cored, seeded, and cut into 1/4-inch dice
1 green bell pepper, cored, seeded, and cut into 1/4-inch dice
1/2 cup chopped fresh cilantro
1/4 cup fresh lime juice (about 2 limes)
1/4 cup unsweetened pineapple juice
2 tablespoons Caribbean-style hot sauce, such as Inner Beauty Real Hot Sauce
Salt and freshly ground black pepper to taste

 In a nonreactive bowl, combine all the ingredients and stir gently. Serve immediately, or store, covered and refrigerated, for up to 3 days.

NOTE: Chris says the hot sauce should be as hot as you can tolerate. Inner Beauty Real Hot Sauce is fiery.

(Overleaf) CHRIS SCHLESINGER:
Spice-Rubbed Swordfish with Mango-Lime Salsa ▷▷

ED BROWN

Striped Bass with Mango-Black Bean Salsa, Chayote Squash, and Mango Sauce

SERVES 6
PREPARATION TIME: ABOUT 1½ HOURS
COOKING TIME: ABOUT 10 MINUTES

FAT PER SERVING: 9.2 GRAMS
SATURATED FAT: 1.6 GRAMS
CALORIES PER SERVING: 273
CALORIES FROM FAT: 31%

The zesty flavors mask the fact that there is not a lot of fat in this easy-to-put-together tropical recipe. You could replace the striped bass with sea bass or grouper.

Six 7-ounce striped bass fillets, skin side scored (see Note)
Coarse salt and freshly ground black pepper to taste
2 tablespoons olive oil
3 chayote squash, peeled, seeded, and cut into julienne
Mango Sauce (recipe follows)
Mango-Black Bean Salsa (recipe follows)

1 Assemble *mise en place* trays for this recipe (see page 6).

2 Season the fish with coarse salt and pepper to taste. In a heavy sauté pan large enough to hold the fish comfortably, heat 1 tablespoon of the oil over medium-high heat. Place the fish skin side down in the pan and cook for 2½ minutes. Turn and cook for about 2½ minutes longer, or until the fish is firm and the flesh is opaque. Remove to a warm platter and cover with foil to keep warm.

3 In another sauté pan, heat the remaining 1 tablespoon oil over medium heat. Add the squash, season to taste with coarse salt and pepper, and sauté for about 3 minutes, or until slightly softened.

4 Place equal portions of squash on each plate and lay a fillet on top. Drizzle the sauce around and spoon about 2 tablespoons of the salsa at the side of each fillet. Serve immediately.

ED BROWN: Striped Bass with Mango–Black Bean Salsa, Chayote Squash, and Mango Sauce

NOTE: To score the bass, use a small sharp knife to lightly cut a crisscross pattern into the skin.

You can cook the squash while the fish is cooking, although it will take some kitchen juggling. You may need to use 2 pans to cook the fish—and another tablespoon of oil.

MANGO SAUCE

MAKES ABOUT 2 CUPS
FAT PER 1/3-CUP SERVING: 5.3 GRAMS
SATURATED FAT: 0.3 GRAM
CALORIES PER SERVING: 71
CALORIES FROM FAT: 63%

2 mangoes, peeled and cubed, or 8 ounces canned mango purée
1/2 cup water
2 tablespoons canola oil
1/4 cup Champagne vinegar
Pinch of cayenne pepper
Salt to taste

In a blender, combine all the ingredients and process for about 3 minutes, or until smooth. Use immediately, or pour into a nonreactive container, cover, and refrigerate for up to 2 days.

MANGO-BLACK BEAN SALSA

MAKES ABOUT 3 CUPS
FAT PER 1/2-CUP SERVING: 1 GRAM
SATURATED FAT: 0.1 GRAM
CALORIES PER SERVING: 84
CALORIES FROM FAT: 10%

2/3 cup finely diced mango (1 to 2 mangoes)
1/3 cup cooked black beans (see page 15)
1/2 red bell pepper, cored, seeded, and cut into 1/4-inch dice
2 scallions, green parts only, chopped
1 orange, peeled and cut into membrane-free segments
1/2 lime, peeled and cut into membrane-free segments
1 tablespoon chopped fresh cilantro
1 1/2 cups fresh orange juice
1 teaspoon rice wine vinegar
1 teaspoon extra-virgin olive oil
1/4 teaspoon red pepper flakes
Salt to taste

Up to 1 hour before serving, combine all the ingredients in a nonreactive bowl. Let stand at room temperature until ready to serve.

NOTE: The recipes makes more salsa than you will need. Cover and refrigerate it for up to 3 days.

ED BROWN

Grilled Swordfish and Fennel with Charred Tomatoes, Oil-Roasted Garlic, and Balsamic Vinegar

SERVES 6
PREPARATION TIME: ABOUT 45 MINUTES
COOKING TIME: ABOUT 40 MINUTES
GRILLING TIME: ABOUT 10 MINUTES

FAT PER SERVING: 10 GRAMS
SATURATED FAT: 2.1 GRAMS
CALORIES PER SERVING: 237
CALORIES FROM FAT: 39%

Ed Brown uses thirty-year-old balsamic vinegar in this dish; if you don't have any on hand, substitute any fine-quality balsamic vinegar for the very expensive "Champagne" variety. Again, this is Ed Brown at his best—great flavor, beautiful presentation, and health-conscious ingredients. His unique way of roasting garlic adds interest to the plate, but because it also adds calories and fat, you may choose to eliminate the garlic garnish.

1 large bulb fennel
3 large beefsteak tomatoes, cored and cut into 4 slices each

2 tablespoons extra-virgin olive oil
1 1/2 teaspoons fresh thyme leaves
Coarse salt and freshly ground black pepper to taste
Six 5-ounce swordfish steaks, at least 3/4 inch thick
3 tablespoons balsamic vinegar
Oil-Roasted Garlic (recipe follows; optional)
1 tablespoon fresh rosemary leaves
6 sprigs fresh rosemary, for garnish

1 Assemble *mise en place* trays for this recipe (see page 6).

2 Trim the fennel and cut lengthwise into 6 slices. Cut a "V" in the bottom of each slice to remove the tough core. Blanch in a saucepan of boiling salted water for 3 minutes, drain, and pat dry. Set aside.

3 Sprinkle the tomatoes with 1 teaspoon of the oil, the

Ed Brown: Grilled Swordfish and Fennel with Charred Tomatoes, Oil-Roasted Garlic, and Balsamic Vinegar

6 Brush the swordfish with the remaining 1 tablespoon oil and season to taste with coarse salt and pepper. Grill over hot coals for about 3 minutes on each side, or until the center is just firm, for medium-rare. If broiling, broil the fennel about 5 inches from the heat and the swordfish closer to the heat source. Using 2 tablespoons of the vinegar, brush the fish on each side.

7 Place a slice of fennel in the center of each plate. Cut each tomato slice in half and arrange 4 pieces of tomato in a pinwheel design around the fennel on each plate. Randomly place 3 roasted garlic cloves on each plate and sprinkle with the rosemary. Drizzle the remaining vinegar over the plates. Cut each fish steak in half on the bias and place on top of the fennel, slightly overlapping the halves. Garnish with the rosemary sprigs and serve immediately.

NOTE: If fresh herbs are not available, do not replace with dried—instead, use chopped parsley for seasoning and garnish.

OIL-ROASTED GARLIC

18 large cloves garlic
3 cups olive oil

In a small nonreactive saucepan, combine the garlic and oil and simmer over low heat for about 40 minutes, or until the garlic is very soft. Drain, reserving the oil for another use, and serve.

thyme, and coarse salt and pepper to taste. Place a nonstick griddle or cast-iron skillet over high heat. When hot, char the tomatoes, a few at a time, for about 30 seconds on each side, until darkened. Set aside.

4 Prepare a charcoal or gas grill or preheat the broiler. Ignite some extra coals and keep them ready in a metal bucket or second grill.

5 Toss the fennel with 2 teaspoons of the oil and coarse salt and pepper to taste. Grill over medium-hot coals for about 2 minutes on each side, or until well colored. Set aside and cover to keep warm. Add the ignited charcoal to the grill to increase the heat.

Sole with Tomato Fondue and Saffron Pasta

SERVES 6
PREPARATION TIME: ABOUT 30 MINUTES
COOKING TIME: ABOUT 40 MINUTES

FAT PER SERVING: 6 GRAMS
SATURATED FAT: 1 GRAM
CALORIES PER SERVING: 420
CALORIES FROM FAT: 15%

Georges normally makes fresh saffron egg pasta for this dish but, in the interest of saving calories, we have substituted more ordinary dried pasta. If you can find saffron-flavored dried pasta, by all means use it.

1 tablespoon toasted saffron threads
1 cup water
1 pound imported dried fettuccine
Salt to taste
Six 4-ounce Dover sole fillets
Salt and freshly ground black pepper to taste
1/4 cup all-purpose flour
2 tablespoons plus 1 teaspoon olive oil
Tomato Fondue (recipe follows)
2 tablespoons chopped fresh chives

1 Assemble *mise en place* trays for this recipe (see page 6).

2 In a small saucepan, combine the saffron and water and bring to a boil over high heat. Reduce the heat and simmer for about 30 minutes, or until the liquid is reduced to 3 tablespoons. Strain, discarding the saffron, and set the liquid aside.

3 Bring a large pot of salted water to a boil over high heat. Add the pasta and cook for about 9 minutes, or until *al dente*.

4 Meanwhile, season the sole with salt and pepper and then lightly dredge with the flour, shaking off the excess. In a nonstick sauté pan large enough to hold the fish comfortably, heat 2 tablespoons of the oil. Cook the sole for about 30 seconds on each side, until opaque. Remove from the heat and cover to keep warm.

5 Drain the pasta and toss with the reserved saffron water, the remaining 1 teaspoon oil, and salt to taste. Place equal portions of the hot pasta in the center of 6 plates. Lay a fillet on top and ladle 3 tablespoons Tomato Fondue over each. Sprinkle with the chives and serve immediately.

NOTE: If you decide to make your own fresh pasta, add the saffron water to the dough rather than using it as a seasoning.

▶ Replace the Dover sole with petrale sole, lemon sole, rex sole, or any other member of the flounder family.

▶ Toast the saffron in a nonstick skillet over medium heat for about 30 seconds, just until fragrant.

TOMATO FONDUE

MAKES ABOUT 2 CUPS
FAT PER 3-TABLESPOON SERVING: 18 GRAMS
SATURATED FAT: 2.4 GRAMS
CALORIES PER SERVING: 204
CALORIES FROM FAT: 78%

8 ripe tomatoes, peeled, cored, seeded, and chopped
1/2 cup extra-virgin olive oil
1/4 cup balsamic vinegar
3 tablespoons chopped fresh flat-leaf parsley
3 tablespoons chopped fresh chives
Coarse salt and freshly ground black pepper to taste

In a medium nonreactive saucepan, combine the tomatoes, oil, and vinegar and bring to a boil over medium-low heat. Cook, stirring frequently, for about 40 minutes, or until thickened and reduced slightly. Remove from the heat and stir in the parsley and chives. Season to taste with coarse salt and pepper. Keep warm until ready to serve.

NOTE: This can be made up to 1 week ahead, covered, and refrigerated. Reheat gently to serve. Reserve leftovers for another use.

(See pages 42–43 for photograph)

DANIEL BOULUD
Broiled Pompano with Pickles and Vegetables

SERVES 6
PREPARATION TIME: ABOUT 40 MINUTES
COOKING TIME: ABOUT 13 MINUTES

FAT PER SERVING: 11 GRAMS
SATURATED FAT: 4.2 GRAMS
CALORIES PER SERVING: 210
CALORIES FROM FAT: 51%

This savory dish explodes with exuberant tastes. The pickle-vegetable garnish offers satisfaction with little fat. The percentage of calories from fat seems high because the calories per serving are low.

2 tablespoons olive oil
2 scallions, minced
1/2 cup finely minced celery
1/4 cup diced zucchini (1/4-inch dice)
1 red bell pepper, roasted, peeled, cored, seeded, and cut into 1/4-inch dice (see page 12)
1 tablespoon capers, preferably French, drained
1 tablespoon coarsely chopped cornichons
1 1/2 teaspoons grated fresh horseradish
2 lemons, peeled and cut into membrane-free segments
2 tablespoons fresh lemon juice
Coarse salt and freshly ground black pepper to taste
Six 4-ounce skinless pompano fillets
1 teaspoon minced fresh thyme
18 small celery leaves, washed and dried, for garnish

1 Assemble *mise en place* trays for this recipe (see page 6).

2 In a medium-sized saucepan, heat 1 1/2 teaspoons of the oil over medium heat. Add the scallions and celery and sauté for about 5 minutes, or until the vegetables soften. Add the zucchini and sauté for 3 minutes. Stir in the roasted pepper, capers, cornichons, horseradish, lemon segments, lemon juice, and 1 1/2 teaspoons of the oil. Season to taste with coarse salt and pepper, remove from the heat, and cover to keep warm.

3 Preheat the broiler.

4 Brush a broiling pan and the fillets with the remaining 1 tablespoon oil. Sprinkle the fish with the thyme and coarse salt and pepper to taste and broil for about 2 1/2 minutes on each side, or until just cooked through.

5 Place a fillet on each warm plate, spoon the warm pickle garnish on top, and garnish each with 3 celery leaves.

DANIEL BOULUD: Broiled Pompano with Pickles and Vegetables

EMERIL LAGASSE
Big Easy Seafood-Okra Gumbo

SERVES 6
PREPARATION TIME: ABOUT 40 MINUTES
COOKING TIME: ABOUT 35 MINUTES

FAT PER SERVING: 7.9 GRAMS
SATURATED FAT: 1.3 GRAMS
CALORIES PER SERVING: 428
CALORIES FROM FAT: 19%

This is a wonderful party dish—rich, aromatic, and filling. Serve it with crisp toasts and a crisp white wine or maybe a light beer.

2 tablespoons plus 1 teaspoon olive oil
2 medium-sized onions, cut into 1/2-inch dice
2 ribs celery, cut into 1/2-inch dice
1 green bell pepper, cored, seeded, and cut into 1/2-inch dice
1 red bell pepper, cored, seeded, and cut into 1/2-inch dice
1 tablespoon minced shallots
1 teaspoon minced garlic
3 plum tomatoes, peeled, seeded, and chopped
1/4 pound okra, trimmed and sliced 1/4 inch thick
8 cups Fish Stock (see page 14)
1/2 pound boneless firm-fleshed fish, such as grouper, bass, or snapper, cut into chunks
1/2 pound shrimp, peeled and deveined
1/4 pound crabmeat, picked over for shells and cartilage
1 tablespoon chopped fresh basil
2 teaspoons chopped fresh oregano
1 teaspoon chopped fresh thyme
2 bay leaves
2 tablespoons Emeril's Creole Seasoning (recipe follows)
2 tablespoons gumbo filé powder
Worcestershire sauce to taste
Tabasco sauce to taste
1 cup shucked oysters, with their liquid
6 cups hot cooked white rice

1 Assemble *mise en place* trays for this recipe (see page 6).

2 In a large saucepan, heat 2 tablespoons of the oil over medium heat. Add the onions, celery, bell peppers, shallots, and garlic and sauté for about 7 minutes, or until the onions are translucent.

3 Stir in the tomatoes and okra and cook for 5 minutes. Add the stock, bring to a simmer, and simmer for about 20 minutes, or until the okra is tender.

EMERIL LAGASSE: Big Easy Seafood-Okra Gumbo

4 Meanwhile, in a large sauté pan, heat the remaining 1 teaspoon oil over medium heat. Add the fish pieces, shrimp, and crab and sauté for about 3 minutes, or until the fish is firm but not cooked through. Drain off the liquid and set the fish and seafood aside.

5 Add the basil, oregano, thyme, bay leaves, Creole seasoning, filé powder, and Worcestershire sauce and Tabasco to taste to the simmering stock and stir to combine. Add the reserved fish and seafood, taste, and adjust the seasonings. Add the oysters with their liquid and cook for about 1 minute, or until they plump.

6 Place equal portions of rice in each shallow bowl. Ladle the gumbo over the top and serve immediately.

NOTE: The gumbo stock base can be made early in the day. Reheat and add the fish and seafood just before serving.

EMERIL'S CREOLE SEASONING

MAKES ABOUT ¾ CUP

2½ tablespoons paprika
2 tablespoons coarse salt

2 tablespoons garlic powder
1 tablespoon freshly ground black pepper
1 tablespoon onion powder
1 tablespoon cayenne pepper
1 tablespoon dried oregano
1 tablespoon dried thyme

In a glass or ceramic container with an airtight lid, combine all the ingredients. Cover and shake well to combine. Store, covered, for up to 6 months.

MARIO BATALI

Fusilli with Twenty-Minute Tomato Sauce, Hot Chiles, and Arugula

SERVES 6
PREPARATION TIME: 10 MINUTES
COOKING TIME: ABOUT 20 MINUTES

FAT PER SERVING: 12.2 GRAMS
SATURATED FAT: 4.2 GRAMS
CALORIES PER SERVING: 475
CALORIES FROM FAT: 23%

Quick, healthy, and delicious—with a touch of heat! What more could the home cook ask? (Except, perhaps to have Mario himself cook it for you!)

½ cup chopped carrots
2 tablespoons olive oil
1 medium onion, finely diced
3 cloves garlic, minced
2 tablespoons balsamic vinegar
2 tablespoons fresh thyme leaves
1 tablespoon red pepper flakes
One-and-one-third 35-ounce boxes strained tomatoes (about 6 cups; see Note)
Salt to taste
1 pound imported dried fusilli pasta
1 bunch arugula, trimmed, washed, dried, and cut into ¼-inch chiffonade
One 2-ounce piece Pecorino-Romano cheese, for grating (optional)

1 Assemble *mise en place* trays for this recipe (see page 6).

2 In a food processor fitted with the metal blade, combine the carrots and oil and process until the carrots are minced. Transfer to a large saucepan, stir in the onions and garlic, and cook over medium heat, stirring frequently, for about 7 minutes, or until the onions begin to brown.

MARIO BATALI: Fusilli with Twenty-Minute Tomato Sauce, Hot Chiles, and Arugula

3 Add the vinegar, thyme, and pepper flakes and cook, stirring, for 1 minute. Add the tomatoes, raise the heat to high, and cook, stirring frequently, for about 8 minutes, or until the sauce thickens slightly. Season to taste with salt. Remove from the heat and cover to keep warm.

4 Meanwhile, bring a large pot of salted water to a boil over high heat. Add the pasta and cook for about 9 minutes, or until *al dente*. Drain, add to the sauce, and toss to combine. Return to the heat for 1 minute, just to heat through.

5 Remove from the heat and toss in the arugula. Pour into a warm serving dish and serve immediately. Grate the cheese over individual servings if desired.

NOTE: Pomi brand produces excellent boxed strained tomatoes.

PAUL BARTOLOTTA

Bow Tie Pasta with Mussels and Zucchini

SERVES 6
PREPARATION TIME: ABOUT 30 MINUTES
COOKING TIME: ABOUT 20 MINUTES

FAT PER SERVING: 11.5 GRAMS
SATURATED FAT: 1.9 GRAMS
CALORIES PER SERVING: 424
CALORIES FROM FAT: 25%

This ambrosial combination of flavors truly is a one-dish meal filled with nutritious goodness.

1 1/2 tablespoons extra-virgin olive oil
1 tablespoon minced garlic
54 mussels, well scrubbed and debearded
2 1/4 cups dry white wine
6 bay leaves
Pinch of red pepper flakes
3 medium-sized zucchini, cut on the diagonal into 1/8-inch-thick slices
6 tomatoes, peeled, cored, seeded, and diced
1 1/2 tablespoons chopped fresh flat-leaf parsley
1 pound imported dried bow tie pasta
Salt and freshly ground black pepper to taste

1 Assemble *mise en place* trays for this recipe (see page 6).

2 In a large saucepan, heat 1 tablespoon of the oil over medium heat. Add the garlic and sauté for 1 minute. Add the mussels, wine, bay leaves, and pepper flakes, cover, and steam for about 5 minutes, or until the mussels open. Using a slotted spoon, transfer the mussels to a bowl. Discard any that have not opened. Bring the broth to a boil over high heat and cook for 3 to 4 minutes to burn off the acidity of the wine. Remove from the heat.

3 In a large sauté pan, heat the remaining 1 1/2 teaspoons oil over medium heat. Add the zucchini and sauté for about 5 minutes, or until slightly softened. Stir in the tomatoes, mussels, and broth, remove from the heat, and set aside.

4 Meanwhile, bring a large pot of salted water to a boil over high heat. Add the pasta and cook for about 10 minutes, or until *al dente*. Drain.

5 Add the pasta to the sauce and heat, stirring constantly, over medium heat for about 3 minutes, or until the natural starch of the pasta thickens the sauce. Add the parsley, season to taste with salt and pepper, and serve immediately.

PATRICIA JAMIESON
Ziti with Lentils and Kale

SERVES 6
PREPARATION TIME: ABOUT 30 MINUTES
COOKING TIME: ABOUT 45 MINUTES

FAT PER SERVING: 6.7 GRAMS
SATURATED FAT: 0.6 GRAM
CALORIES PER SERVING: 490
CALORIES FROM FAT: 12%

Lentils make this sauce so robust that it becomes an interesting alternative to long-simmered more traditional sauces. Large pasta shapes, such as ziti, fusilli, or rotini, are ideal because the lentils nestle in their holes and crevices.

1/2 cup green lentils, preferably Le Puy
11/2 teaspoons olive oil
1 medium-sized onion, chopped
1 medium-sized carrot, chopped
4 cloves garlic, minced
2 ounces prosciutto, trimmed of fat and chopped (about 1/4 cup)
2 cups Chicken Broth (see page 14)
1 teaspoon chopped fresh rosemary or pinch of dried
1 teaspoon fresh thyme leaves or 1/2 teaspoon dried
One 28-ounce can plum tomatoes, drained and chopped
4 cups coarsely chopped kale (about 1/2 bunch)
Salt and freshly ground black pepper to taste
1 pound imported dried ziti
1/4 cup freshly grated Parmigiano-Reggiano cheese (optional)

1 Assemble *mise en place* trays for this recipe (see page 6).

2 In a medium-sized saucepan, cover the lentils with cold water, bring to a boil over high heat, and boil for 5 minutes to soften. Remove from the heat, drain, rinse under cold running water, and set aside.

3 In a nonstick sauté pan, heat the oil over medium heat. Add the onions, carrots, garlic, and prosciutto and sauté for about 5 minutes, or until the vegetables soften. Stir in the lentils, add the broth and herbs, and bring to a boil. Reduce the heat, cover, and simmer for about 15 minutes. Add the tomatoes and kale and simmer for an additional 20 minutes, or until the lentils and kale are tender. Season to taste with salt and pepper.

PATRICIA JAMIESON: Ziti with Lentils and Kale

4 Meanwhile, bring a large pot of salted water to a boil over high heat. Add the pasta and cook for about 10 minutes, or until *al dente*. Drain and transfer to a large warm shallow bowl.

5 Add the sauce to the pasta and toss to combine. Taste and adjust the seasonings with salt and pepper. Serve immediately, passing the cheese on the side if desired.

MARIE SIMMONS

Orecchiette with Zucchini and Yellow Squash

SERVES 6
PREPARATION TIME: ABOUT 15 MINUTES
COOKING TIME: ABOUT 10 MINUTES

FAT PER SERVING: 4.3 GRAMS
SATURATED FAT: 0.5 GRAM
CALORIES PER SERVING: 331
CALORIES FROM FAT: 12%

Since both zucchini and yellow squash are very moist, they require very little cooking. If you undercook the vegetables slightly, the hot pasta and the addition of a little of the boiling pasta water will complete the cooking yet allow the vegetables to retain their bright color and crispness. A light dusting of robustly flavored Parmigiano-Reggiano or Pecorino Romano cheese provides a blast of flavor with a minimum of fat and calories. This serves as a very light and graceful *primi piatti,* or first-course pasta dish, as well as a simple main course.

1 pound imported dried orecchiette pasta
1 tablespoon olive oil
2 scallions, chopped
1 clove garlic, minced
3 medium-sized zucchini, thinly sliced
2 yellow squash, thinly sliced
1 tablespoon freshly grated Parmigiano-Reggiano or Pecorino Romano cheese, plus, if desired, additional for serving
Salt and freshly ground black pepper to taste

1 Assemble *mise en place* trays for this recipe (see page 6).

2 Bring a large pot of salted water to a boil over high heat. Add the pasta and cook for about 10 minutes, or until *al dente.* Scoop out ½ cup of the cooking water and set it aside, then drain the pasta.

3 Meanwhile, in a medium-sized sauté pan, heat the oil over medium heat. Add the scallions and garlic and sauté for 2 minutes. Add the zucchini and yellow squash and sauté for about 3 minutes, or until the vegetables just begin to soften. Add the pasta, the reserved pasta cooking water, and the cheese and toss to coat. Season to taste with salt and pepper. Spoon into warm pasta bowls and, if desired, offer additional cheese on the side.

MARIE SIMMONS: Orecchiette with Zucchini and Yellow Squash

Desserts

Grilled Peaches with Blue Cheese and Sweet Balsamic Vinegar Glaze

Banana-Pineapple Shake

Baked Peaches with Warm Blueberry-Thyme Sauce

Apricots Baked with Kirsch and Vanilla

Plum and Ginger Kuchen

Roasted Caramelized Pears

Blackberry-Rhubarb Phyllo Tart

Dried Fig and Apricot Tart

Carrot-Raisin Cake

Pumpkin Crème Brûlée

◁◁ (Overleaf) MARIE SIMMONS: Dried Fig and Apricot Tart

CHRIS SCHLESINGER

Grilled Peaches with Blue Cheese and Sweet Balsamic Vinegar Glaze

SERVES 6
PREPARATION TIME: ABOUT 15 MINUTES
COOKING TIME: ABOUT 40 MINUTES

FAT PER SERVING, WITH BLUE CHEESE: 10 GRAMS
SATURATED FAT: 4.1 GRAMS
CALORIES PER SERVING: 205
CALORIES FROM FAT: 43%

FAT PER SERVING, WITH LOW-FAT SOUR CREAM: 0.3 GRAM
SATURATED FAT: 0.6 GRAM
CALORIES PER SERVING: 161
CALORIES FROM FAT: 33%

CHRIS SCHLESINGER: Grilled Peaches with Blue Cheese and Sweet Balsamic Vinegar Glaze

This sensual dessert can also be served as an appetizer. If you are counting fat grams closely, eliminate the blue cheese and replace it with a dollop of low-fat sour cream.

1 cup fine-quality balsamic vinegar
2 tablespoons granulated sugar
1 tablespoon coarsely cracked black pepper
5 peaches, halved and pitted
2 tablespoons olive oil
4 ounces blue cheese, crumbled, or ¼ cup plus 2 tablespoons low-fat sour cream

1 Assemble *mise en place* trays for this recipe (see page 6).

2 In a small saucepan, combine the vinegar, sugar, and pepper and bring to a boil over medium heat. Reduce the heat and simmer, stirring occasionally, for about 35 minutes, or until reduced by about two thirds and thick enough to coat the back of a spoon. Set the glaze aside.

3 Preheat a charcoal or gas grill or preheat the broiler.

4 Rub the cut surfaces of the peach halves with the oil and grill, cut side down, over medium coals for about 5 minutes, or until just slightly charred. Alternatively, broil 5 to 6 inches from the heat source. Using a pastry brush, coat the top of each peach with the glaze and grill or broil for another minute, or until the glaze begins to caramelize. Remove from the heat.

5 Brush the peaches with the glaze again and cut into thick slices. Arrange on warm plates and sprinkle with the blue cheese, or top with the sour cream. Serve immediately.

DANIEL BOULUD
Banana-Pineapple Shake

SERVES 6
PREPARATION TIME: ABOUT 15 MINUTES
FREEZING TIME: ABOUT 1 HOUR

FAT PER SERVING: 1.2 GRAMS
SATURATED FAT: 0.1 GRAM
CALORIES PER SERVING: 103
CALORIES FROM FAT: 10%

This exceptionally light dessert is served in Champagne glasses with sprigs of mint. It's equally delicious as a refreshing mid-afternoon snack, for two. Daniel uses sugar substitute in this recipe rather than granulated sugar because its sweetening power is so much greater—a little goes a long way!

1 small pineapple, peeled, cored, and cut into chunks
2 ripe bananas, cut into chunks
1 cup ice-cold 1% milk
2 tablespoons fresh lime juice
1 teaspoon sugar substitute, such as Equal
Grated zest of 1 lime
6 sprigs fresh mint or small pineapple leaves, for garnish

1 Assemble *mise en place* trays for this recipe (see page 6).

2 In a nonreactive freezer-proof container, combine the pineapple and bananas and freeze for 1 hour, or until firm.

3 In a blender, combine the frozen fruit, milk, lime juice, sugar substitute, and lime zest and process until thick and smooth. Serve immediately in frosted Champagne or tall glasses, garnished with the mint sprigs.

NOTE: To frost glasses, place in the freezer for about an hour.

SALLY SCHNEIDER
Baked Peaches with Warm Blueberry-Thyme Sauce

SERVES 6
PREPARATION TIME: ABOUT 20 MINUTES
BAKING TIME: ABOUT 20 MINUTES
COOKING TIME (SAUCE ONLY): ABOUT 5 MINUTES

FAT PER SERVING: 0
SATURATED FAT: 0
CALORIES PER SERVING: 81
CALORIES FROM FAT: 0%

Here is the taste of warm peach and blueberry pie without the "no-no" rich pie crust. I promise you won't miss it! But if you want to splurge, serve a few butter cookies with the peaches.

6 very ripe medium peaches, halved, pitted, and cut into 6 slices each
1 tablespoon fresh lemon juice
1/4 cup plus 2 tablespoons granulated sugar
1 vanilla bean
1/4 cup plus 1 tablespoon water
Warm Blueberry-Thyme Sauce (recipe follows)
1/4 cup plus 2 tablespoons vanilla nonfat yogurt or vanilla non-fat frozen yogurt

1 Assemble *mise en place* trays for this recipe (see page 6). Preheat the oven to 450 degrees F.

2 Lay the peach slices in a 10-inch glass pie plate or round baking dish and drizzle the lemon juice over the fruit.

SALLY SCHNEIDER: Baked Peaches with Warm Blueberry-Thyme Sauce

◁ **DANIEL BOULUD:** Banana-Pineapple Shake

3 Put the sugar in a small bowl. Split the vanilla bean in half lengthwise and, using a small paring knife, scrape the seeds into the sugar; reserve the bean. Stir to combine and then sprinkle over the peaches.

4 Cut the vanilla bean into 2-inch pieces. Nestle the pieces among the peaches.

5 Add the water to the dish and bake for 10 minutes. Baste the peaches with the accumulated pan juices and bake for an additional 10 minutes, or until the peaches are very tender and the pan juices are thick and syrupy. Baste the peaches again.

6 Pour the Warm Blueberry-Thyme Sauce into shallow bowls and spoon the peach slices into the center of each. Garnish each with 1 tablespoon yogurt. Serve immediately.

NOTE: The peaches can be baked early in the day and held at room temperature until ready to serve.

WARM BLUEBERRY-THYME SAUCE

MAKES ABOUT 2 CUPS
FAT PER 1/3-CUP SERVING: 0.2 GRAM
SATURATED FAT: 0
CALORIES PER SERVING: 59
PERCENTAGE OF FAT PER SERVING: 4%

3 cups fresh blueberries (about 1 pint)
2 tablespoons honey
2 tablespoons water
2 sprigs fresh thyme
1/2 vanilla bean, split

In a small saucepan, combine all the ingredients and cook over medium heat for about 5 minutes, or until the berries release their juices but are still whole. Discard the vanilla bean and serve warm.

NOTE: The sauce can be made with blackberries or raspberries. It can be made up to 3 days ahead, covered, and refrigerated. Reheat gently before serving.

SALLY SCHNEIDER

Apricots Baked with Kirsch and Vanilla

SERVES 6
PREPARATION TIME: ABOUT 10 MINUTES
BAKING TIME: ABOUT 30 MINUTES

FAT PER SERVING: 0.4 GRAM
SATURATED FAT: 0.03 GRAM
CALORIES PER SERVING: 205
CALORIES FROM FAT: 2%

You don't need perfect apricots to make this dish—the vanilla sugar and kirsch magically bring out the hidden assets of the fruit. But make sure the apricots are ripe.

18 ripe apricots, well washed
1/4 cup plus 2 tablespoons superfine sugar
1 vanilla bean
1/2 cup water
2 1/2 tablespoons kirschwasser

1 Assemble *mise en place* trays for this recipe (see page 6). Preheat the oven to 325 degrees F.

2 With a sharp paring knife, make an incision along the natural seam of each apricot, but do not cut all the way around. Gently pry the halves apart, taking care not to separate them completely. Carefully pry out the pits with your fingers and set the apricots aside.

3 Put the sugar in a small bowl. Split the vanilla bean in half lengthwise and, using a small paring knife, scrape the seeds into the sugar; reserve the bean. Stir to combine. Spoon 1/2 teaspoon into the cavity of each apricot. In a shallow 1 1/2-quart baking dish or a glass pie plate, arrange the apricots cut side up, so they fit snugly.

4 Sprinkle the water, kirsch, and remaining vanilla sugar over the apricots. Cut the vanilla bean into 2-inch pieces and nestle the pieces among the apricots.

5 Bake for 15 minutes. Baste the apricots with the accumulated pan juices and bake for an additional 15 minutes, or until the apricots are tender. Cool to room temperature. Serve at room temperature or chilled.

NOTE: This can be made early in the day and held at room temperature until ready to serve. Or cover and refrigerate if you wish to serve the apricots chilled.

SALLY SCHNEIDER: Apricots Baked with Kirsch and Vanilla ▷

MARIE SIMMONS
Plum and Ginger Kuchen

MAKES ONE 9-INCH CAKE; SERVES 6
PREPARATION TIME: ABOUT 20 MINUTES
BAKING TIME: ABOUT 1 HOUR

FAT PER SERVING: 2.3 GRAMS
SATURATED FAT: 0.6 GRAM
CALORIES PER SERVING: 283
CALORIES FROM FAT: 7%

MARIE SIMMONS: Plum and Ginger Kuchen

There is no butter or oil in this old-fashioned fruit dessert. Enjoy it with a scoop of nonfat ice cream or frozen yogurt.

1 pound red plums, washed, halved, pitted, and cut into small pieces
1 cup granulated sugar
1 teaspoon grated fresh ginger
2 large eggs, at room temperature
2 large egg whites, at room temperature
1 teaspoon pure vanilla extract
3/4 cup sifted all-purpose flour
1/4 cup sifted cornstarch
1 teaspoon baking powder

1 Assemble *mise en place* trays for this recipe (see page 6). Preheat the oven to 350 degrees F. Lightly spray a 9-inch springform pan with nonstick vegetable spray.

2 In a bowl, combine the plums, 1/4 cup of the sugar, and 1/2 teaspoon of the ginger and toss to combine. Arrange in an even layer in the prepared pan and set aside.

3 In a large bowl, using an electric mixer, beat the eggs, egg whites, and vanilla for about 2 minutes, or until foamy. Gradually add the remaining 3/4 cup sugar and beat for about 4 minutes, or until the mixture is pale yellow and thick. Beat in the remaining 1/2 teaspoon ginger.

4 Sift the flour, cornstarch, and baking powder onto the egg mixture and gently fold in with rubber spatula just until all the flour is incorporated. Carefully spread the batter over the plums.

5 Bake for about 1 hour, or until the top of the cake is browned and the center feels firm to the touch. Cool on a wire rack.

6 When cool, run a small knife around the sides of the pan and remove the rim of the springform pan. Invert the cake onto a serving platter and serve at room temperature.

SALLY SCHNEIDER
Roasted Caramelized Pears

SERVES 6
PREPARATION TIME: ABOUT 10 MINUTES
BAKING TIME: ABOUT 45 MINUTES

FAT PER SERVING: 1.5 GRAMS
SATURATED FAT: 0.8 GRAM
CALORIES PER SERVING: 88
CALORIES FROM FAT: 15%

This rich-tasting dessert is so satisfying, yet it's low in fat and calories. That makes it easy to enjoy without guilt.

3 medium-sized pears (about 1 pound), peeled, cut lengthwise in half, and cored
2/3 cup sweet dessert wine, such as Muscat de Beaumes-de-Venise, Sauternes, or Barsac
1 vanilla bean
2 teaspoons unsalted butter
1 tablespoon granulated sugar

1 Assemble *mise en place* trays for this recipe (see page 6). Preheat the oven to 375 degrees F.

2 Arrange the pears cut side up in a 10-inch glass pie plate or baking dish.

3 Put the wine in a small bowl. Split the vanilla bean in half lengthwise and, using a small paring knife, scrape the beans into the wine. Stir to combine and pour over the fruit. (Discard the bean or save it for another use.)

4 Dot the pears with the butter and bake for 20 minutes, basting occasionally with the accumulated pan juices. Turn the pears and sprinkle with the sugar. Bake, basting frequently, for an additional 25 minutes, or until the pears are glazed and golden. If the pan juices evaporate too quickly, add warm water, a tablespoon at a time, to the pan. Cool slightly, then baste once more with the syrup and serve warm.

NOTE: These can be made early in the day, covered, refrigerated, and reheated just before serving. Bring them to room temperature before reheating in a 350-degree-F oven for about 10 minutes.

SALLY SCHNEIDER: Roasted Caramelized Pears

PATRICIA JAMIESON
Blackberry-Rhubarb Phyllo Tart

MAKES ONE 9-INCH TART; SERVES 6
PREPARATION TIME: ABOUT 40 MINUTES
COOKING TIME: ABOUT 2 MINUTES
BAKING TIME: ABOUT 50 MINUTES

FAT PER SERVING: 10 GRAMS
SATURATED FAT: 2.9 GRAMS
CALORIES PER SERVING: 308
CALORIES FROM FAT: 28%

This is delicious made with summer's freshest fruit, but it works almost as well with frozen fruit. You don't need to thaw the fruit, but in that case, bake the tart for an additional twenty minutes or so. This is delicious served with low-fat ice cream.

1 pound rhubarb, trimmed and cut into 1-inch pieces (about 3 cups)
2 cups fresh blackberries
¾ cup plus 2 tablespoons granulated sugar
1 tablespoon quick-cooking tapioca
2 teaspoons grated lemon zest
2 tablespoons unsalted butter
2 tablespoons vegetable oil, preferably canola

1 large egg white, at room temperature
Six 14 × 18-inch sheets phyllo dough, thawed according to package instructions
1 tablespoon plus 2 teaspoons fine dry bread crumbs
About 2 tablespoons confectioners' sugar, for dusting

1 Assemble *mise en place* trays for this recipe (see page 6). Set the oven rack on the lowest level and preheat the oven to 400 degrees F. Place a heavy-duty baking sheet on the rack to heat. Spray a 9-inch pie plate with nonstick vegetable spray.

2 In a large bowl, combine the rhubarb, berries, sugar, tapioca, and lemon zest and toss to blend. Set aside.

3 In a small saucepan, melt the butter over very low heat. Skim off any foam that rises to the surface and cook for about 2 minutes, or until the butter begins to turn a light,

PATRICIA JAMIESON:
Blackberry-Rhubarb
Phyllo Tart

nutty brown. Take care not to burn. Pour into a small bowl and set aside to cool.

4 When the butter is cool, use a fork to whisk in the oil and egg white until well blended.

5 Lay 1 sheet of the thawed phyllo in the prepared pie plate so that the edges hang over the sides. (As you work, keep the sheets of phyllo not being immediately used covered with a damp kitchen towel.) With a pastry brush, brush the phyllo with the egg white mixture. Sprinkle with 1 teaspoon of the bread crumbs. Lay another sheet of phyllo at an angle over the first. Brush with the egg white mixture and sprinkle with 1 teaspoon bread crumbs. Repeat with 3 more sheets of phyllo, brushing with the egg mixture and sprinkling with the crumbs.

6 Spoon the fruit mixture into the phyllo-lined pie plate. Lift a section of the overhanging phyllo, give it a twist, and drape it over the fruit filling to form a ruffle. Repeat with the remaining overhanging phyllo, lifting it at 4 points in all. Brush the ruffled phyllo with the egg white mixture.

Lay the remaining sheet of phyllo on a sheet of wax paper and cut it in half lengthwise and then crosswise. Lift each quarter from underneath, bunch it together at the center to form a ruffle, and place it over the exposed fruit in the center of the tart to give the entire tart a ruffled top. (Do not worry if some fruit is still visible; small openings serve as steam vents.) Brush the center ruffles with the egg white mixture.

7 Set the pie plate on the baking sheet in the oven and bake for 10 minutes. Reduce the heat to 350 degrees F and bake for 40 to 50 minutes longer, or until the pastry is golden and the fruit mixture is bubbling. Cool to room temperature on a wire rack.

8 Just before serving, dust the top with confectioners' sugar.

NOTE: The tart is best served the day it is made. If the phyllo ruffles soften, reheat the tart in a 350-degree-F oven to crisp them.

MARIE SIMMONS
Dried Fig and Apricot Tart

MAKES ONE 9-INCH TART; SERVES 8
PREPARATION TIME: ABOUT 30 MINUTES
COOKING TIME: ABOUT 25 MINUTES
CHILLING TIME: ABOUT 1 HOUR AND 15
  MINUTES
BAKING TIME: ABOUT 40 MINUTES

FAT PER SERVING: 12.2 GRAMS
SATURATED FAT: 1.2 GRAMS
CALORIES PER SERVING: 461
CALORIES FROM FAT: 23%

To reduce saturated fat, the pastry crust is made with vegetable oil instead of butter. It gets its distinctive, aromatic flavor from cinnamon. This tart is reminiscent of a classic Italian tart called a *crostata*.

1 1/2 cups diced dried figs
1/4 cup diced dried apricots
1/4 cup golden raisins
2 cups water
1 cinnamon stick
2 teaspoons pure vanilla extract
2 cups all-purpose flour
1/4 cup granulated sugar
1 teaspoon ground cinnamon plus a pinch
1/2 teaspoon salt
1/3 cup vegetable oil, preferably canola
1/3 cup plus 1 tablespoon 1% milk
1 tablespoon confectioners' sugar

■ Special Equipment: 9-inch tart pan with a removable bottom

1 Assemble *mise en place* trays for this recipe (see page 6).

2 In a medium-sized saucepan, combine the figs, apricots, raisins, water, and cinnamon stick and bring to a boil over medium-high heat. Reduce the temperature to medium and simmer, stirring frequently, for about 25 minutes, or until the fruit is soft and the water is absorbed. (Add more water if it evaporates too quickly during cooking.) The mixture should be very thick. Cool slightly, then remove the cinnamon stick and stir in the vanilla. Spread on a plate and refrigerate for at least 1 hour, or until stiff.

3 In a large bowl, whisk together the flour, sugar, 1 teaspoon of the cinnamon, and the salt. In a glass measuring cup, stir together the oil and 1/3 cup of the milk. Slowly add to the dry ingredients, stirring constantly with a fork. Gather the dough into a disc, wrap in a plastic wrap, and refrigerate for at least 15 minutes, or until cold.

4 Preheat the oven to 425 degrees F.

5 Divide the dough in half. Roll each piece between 2 sheets of wax paper to an 11-inch round. Fit 1 round into a 9-inch tart pan with a removable bottom. Spread the fig mixture over the dough. Top with the remaining round of dough. Trim the edges and crimp the top and bottom crusts together. Using a small sharp knife, cut several steam vents in the top crust. If desired, cut leaves or other design from the scraps of dough and decorate the top crust. Brush the crust with the remaining 1 tablespoon milk.

6 Bake for 15 minutes. Reduce the heat to 350 degrees F and bake for about 35 minutes longer, or until the pastry is lightly browned. Cool completely on a wire rack.

7 Remove the tart ring and place the tart on a serving platter. In a small bowl, combine the confectioners' sugar and pinch of cinnamon. Transfer to a small strainer, sift over the top of the tart, and serve.

(See pages 74–75 for photograph)

JANE BRODY
Carrot-Raisin Cake

MAKES ONE 9-INCH LOAF; SERVES 6
PREPARATION TIME: ABOUT 30 MINUTES
BAKING TIME: ABOUT 1 HOUR

FAT PER SERVING: 9.6 GRAMS
SATURATED FAT: 1 GRAM
CALORIES PER SERVING: 415
CALORIES FROM FAT: 21%

Jane Brody's "almost-good-for-you" carrot cake has such a wonderful, moist texture and satisfying flavor, no one will guess that it is so low in saturated fat.

1 1/2 teaspoons baking soda
1/4 cup warm water
1 1/2 cups finely shredded carrots
1 cup raisins
1/2 cup plain nonfat yogurt
1/2 cup granulated sugar, or to taste
1/2 cup unsweetened applesauce
1/4 cup vegetable oil, preferably canola
2 large egg whites
2 teaspoons ground cinnamon
1/2 teaspoon grated nutmeg
1/2 teaspoon ground cloves
1/2 teaspoon salt (optional)
1 cup whole wheat flour
1 cup all-purpose flour

1 Assemble *mise en place* trays for this recipe (see page 6). Preheat the oven the 325 degrees F. Lightly spray a 9 x 5-inch loaf pan with nonstick vegetable spray.

2 In a small bowl, combine the baking soda and warm water and set aside.

JANE BRODY: Carrot-Raisin Cake

3 In a large bowl, combine the carrots, raisins, yogurt, sugar, applesauce, oil, egg whites, cinnamon, nutmeg, cloves, and the salt, if desired. Stir in the flours and then stir in the baking soda mixture just until combined.

4 Pour the batter into prepared pan and bake for about 1 hour, or until a toothpick or cake tester inserted into the center comes out clean. Cool in the pan on a wire rack for about 10 minutes before turning the cake out onto the rack to cool completely.

RON HOOK
Pumpkin Crème Brûlée

SERVES 6
PREPARATION TIME: ABOUT 10 MINUTES
BAKING TIME: ABOUT 45 MINUTES

FAT PER SERVING: 2 GRAMS
SATURATED FAT: 1.2 GRAMS
CALORIES PER SERVING: 129
CALORIES FROM FAT: 14%

This is a very light crème brûlée, so we have allowed almost a cup per person. You can, of course, prepare smaller portions to save on calories and fat.

10 large egg whites, at room temperature
1 cup canned pumpkin purée
¼ cup granulated sugar
1 cup evaporated skim milk
2 tablespoons heavy cream
2 teaspoons cornstarch
1 teaspoon pumpkin pie seasoning
⅛ teaspoon salt

1 Assemble *mise en place* trays for this recipe (see page 6). Preheat the oven to 300 degrees F.

2 In a large bowl, combine the egg whites, pumpkin, and sugar and whisk until well blended. Whisk in the milk, cream, cornstarch, pumpkin pie seasoning, and salt.

3 Pour into six 8-ounce glass or ceramic custard cups or ramekins. Place the dishes in a shallow baking dish large enough to hold them comfortably and add enough hot water to come halfway up the sides of the filled dishes.

4 Bake for about 45 minutes, or until the centers are set. Remove the custard cups from the water bath and cool on a wire rack. Serve warm, at room temperature, or chilled.

NOTE: These can be made early in the day, held in the refrigerator, and served chilled or at room temperature. Be sure to use plain pumpkin purée, not sweetened, spiced pumpkin pie filling.

RON HOOK: Pumpkin Crème Brûlée

Suggested Menus

I have assembled some menus to help you plan parties from informal get-togethers to more elaborate affairs using the fresh, healthful recipes in the book. In a few instances, I also recommend easy preparations not included in the book, such as tossed salads and sliced tomatoes. You may want to mix and match other recipes—these are suggestions only.

AN ELEGANT DINNER PARTY

Sweet Pepper and Yellow Pepper Soup*

Roasted Salmon with Moroccan Barbecue Sauce*

Couscous and Sautéed Savoy Cabbage*

Apricots Baked with Kirsch and Vanilla*

A LIGHT AND LIVELY LUNCH

Smothered Escarole on Whole Wheat Crostini*

Orecchiette with Zucchini and Yellow Squash*

Roasted Caramelized Pears*

SUPER SUNDAY SUPPER

Caramelized Onion Pizza*

Appaloosa, Butterscotch, and Chestnut Bean Salad*

Blackberry-Rhubarb Phyllo Tart*

GUILT-FREE COCKTAIL MUNCHIES

Asparagus and Morel Bruschetta*

Intercontinental Chickpea Spread* with Pita Toasts

Shrimp Ceviche*

Parsley Salad with Bulgur, Mint, and Tomatoes* in Hollowed-out Cherry Tomatoes

A LIGHTWEIGHT BUFFET

Braised Wild Mushrooms with Roasted Garlic Toasts*

Big Easy Seafood-Okra Gumbo*

A Big Tossed Green Salad

Dried Fig and Apricot Tart*

HAPPY HEALTHY HOLIDAYS

Eggplant and Crab Garbure with Cumin and Tomato Confit*

Roasted Turkey Breast with Port and Dried Cranberries*

Roasted Sweet Potatoes*

Wild Rice-Orzo Pilaf*

Gingered Green Bean Salad*

LAZY SUMMER PICNIC FOR A CROWD

Chilled Curried Tomato Soup with Cilantro Cream*

Grilled Honey-Basil Chicken*

Spice-Rubbed Swordfish with Mango-Lime Salsa*

Smothered Escarole* (as a side dish)

Corn on the Cob

Sliced Farm-Fresh Tomatoes

A Tray of Summer's Best Fresh Fruits

A WORK NIGHT'S SUPPER

Herb-Marinated Chicken, Shiitake Mushrooms, and Roasted Potato Vinaigrette on Salad Greens*

Banana-Pineapple Shake*

*An asterisk indicates that the recipe is included in this book.

Glossary

Al dente: Italian term meaning, literally, "to the tooth." Most often used to describe pasta that has been cooked until it is just tender but still offers some resistance when chewed. Can also be used to describe the degree to which certain vegetables should be cooked.

Arrowroot: Tasteless, powdery starch derived from a tropical tuber (of the same name), used to thicken sauces, creamy desserts, and pastry fillings, as well as other foods. Arrowroot is used as a flour in some cookies and crackers. It has twice the thickening power of wheat flour.

Arugula: An astringent, fragrant salad green with a sharp, peppery flavor. Also known as rocket and rucola. Highly perishable.

Baba ghanoosh: A Middle Eastern appetizer made from puréed eggplant, sesame seed paste (tahini), olive oil, garlic, and lemon juice.

Balsamic vinegar: Italian specialty vinegar that has been produced in Modena for centuries. It is made from the boiled-down must of white grapes. True balsamic vinegar is aged for decades in a succession of different types of wood barrels.

Blanch: To plunge food briefly into boiling water to set color, texture, or both, or to help loosen the skin. Usually, the food is immediately placed in cold or ice water to stop the cooking process.

Boniato: A white sweet potato-like tuber used extensively in Latin American and Asian cooking. Also called batata or Cuban sweet potato. Available in Latin and Asian markets, as well as some supermarkets.

Braise: To, sometimes but not always, brown meat (or vegetables) first, usually in fat, and then to cook slowly, covered, in a small amount of liquid for a long period of time. Primarily done to tenderize inexpensive cuts of meat.

Bruschetta: Italian bread rubbed with garlic cloves and drizzled with extra-virgin olive oil after being toasted or grilled. Brushetta is always served warm, and may be topped with an assortment of other ingredients, such as tomatoes and cheese.

Bulgur wheat: Steamed, dried, and crushed wheat berries, used extensively in Middle Eastern cooking. Available in coarse, medium, and fine grinds. Sold in natural food stores, specialty shops, and many supermarkets.

Butterfly: To split an ingredient, such as meat or shrimp, in half down the center without cutting completely through it. The two halves are opened like a book to form a butterfly shape.

Ceviche (also seviche): A Latin American dish in which very fresh raw seafood is "cooked" by marinating it in citrus juices. The acidic content of the juice serves to solidify the flesh and turn it opaque. Vegetables are often added to the marinade for color and texture.

Chayote: A mild, thin-skinned, pale green squash that can be eaten raw or cooked. It is pear-shaped with a white interior, and is also known as christophene or mirliton.

Chiffonade: A preparation of greens, classically sorrel, chicory, or lettuce, cut into strips of varying degrees of thickness, easily done by rolling the leaves up cigar-fashion and slicing crosswise. Used as a garnish for soups and cold hors d'oeuvres.

Cilantro: Pungent herb that looks like flat-leaf parsley, used to flavor Asian, Indian, Latin American, and other dishes. The bright green leaves are sometimes referred to as Chinese parsley or fresh coriander. Cilantro is widely available. There is no substitute. Do not use coriander seeds instead!

Confit: Traditionally, a preserved pork, duck, or goose dish whereby the meat is salted and then slowly cooked in its own fat. After cooking, the fat serves as a preservative seal when the mixture is packed into a container and cooled. The term *confit* is now used by many chefs to describe fruits or vegetables that have been slowly cooked in their own juices, often with herbs added.

Couscous: Granular semolina that is a staple of North Africa, particularly Morocco. The term also refers to a dish for which a meat and/or vegetable stew is cooked in the bottom of a *couscousière* (the special pot used only for this dish) while the couscous it will top steams in the perforated upper half.

Cornichon: An imported French gherkin made from tiny pickled cucumbers. Very sour and crisp. Often used as a garnish for pâtés or smoked meats.

Crème fraîche: In France, thickened, unpasteurized cream; in America, pasteurized cream thickened with added fermenting agents. Tastes rather like slightly sweet sour cream.

Crostini: Thick slices of toasted bread, usually from a rustic peasant loaf.

Emulsify: To slowly whisk together two ingredients (such as oil and vinegar) that would not normally blend easily to create a smooth, thick mixture (such as a salad dressing).

Extra-virgin olive oil: Oil from the cold-pressed first pressing of olives, which yields the purest olive taste. Ranging in color from bright green to pale yellow, it is highly flavored and the most expensive olive oil.

Farfalle: Butterfly- or bow tie-shaped pasta.

Fennel: A licorice-scented plant having a bulbous base, celery-like ribs, and feathery foliage. Used extensively in Mediterranean cooking for its sweetly aromatic anise flavor.

Flageolet: Very small, pale green beans grown in France. Usually purchased dried and available in specialty markets.

Frisée: A tangy, curly-leafed endive relative, often called curly endive. Its pale green leaves are used in salads.

Guava: Sweet, oval tropical fruit usually about 2 inches in diameter. Outer skin may range from yellow to red to nearly black, while the flesh is pale yellow to deep red. Available fresh in green-grocers and some gourmet specialty shops. It is also available as a paste, jam, or sauce in specialty food stores and Hispanic markets.

Julienne: Refers to ingredients, particularly vegetables, that have been cut into uniform thin strips, usually about the size of a matchstick. The vegetable to be julienned is first cut into slices of uniform thickness and then the slices are stacked and cut into even strips. Classically, these strips are 1 to 2 inches long by 1/4 inch thick. Usually used as a decorative garnish. See page 12 for instructions for preparing julienne.

Kalamata olive: A large, purple-black Greek olive cured in a wine or vinegar brine and packed in oil or vinegar.

Kirschwasser: A clear brandy distilled from cherry juice and cherry pits. Also called kirsch.

Le Puy lentils: Dusky green, dried French lentils with the seed coat intact.

Orzo: Small rice-shaped pasta.

Parmigiano-Reggiano cheese: Grainy, hard, dry, pale amber Italian part-skim cow's milk cheese with a sharp-sweet taste. Parmigiano-Reggiano is the most eminent of all Parmesan cheeses; its name is always stamped on the rind of cheeses produced in the areas surrounding the Parma and Reggio Emilia regions.

Pecorino Romano cheese: Grainy, hard, dry, aged Italian sheep's milk cheese ranging in color from white to soft yellow, with a very pungent flavor. The best known of the pecorino (sheep) cheeses, it is generally grated for use in cooking and can be substituted for grated Parmesan cheese in many recipes; however, less is called for since it has a sharper taste.

Phyllo (also filo): Tissue paper-thin Greek pastry dough, usually buttered and stacked in layers to enclose sweet or savory mixtures. Available frozen in most supermarkets.

Pilaf: A rice or wheat pasta dish in which the rice or pasta is first browned in oil and then cooked in a well-seasoned broth. Often aromatics, herbs, vegetables, or even meats or fish are added. May be either an entrée or side dish.

Polenta: Cornmeal that has been cooked in either water or stock and is eaten either as a mush or allowed to firm up and then grilled or fried. Often flavored with cheese. May be served as an entrée or a side dish.

Porcini mushrooms: Meaty wild mushrooms of the Boletus edulis species, ranging in size from less than an ounce to more than a pound. Also known as cèpes, porcini are often sold dried.

Quinoa: Ancient, highly nutritional grain from the Andes Mountains in South America that is now being cultivated in small amounts here. Can often be used in recipes calling for other grains. Available in health food stores.

Ragout: A thick, highly seasoned stew.

Rice wine vinegar: A mild Asian vinegar made from fermented rice.

Scotch bonnet: A chile related to the habanero but smaller. Sold fresh, in bright colors ranging from green to yellow, orange, and red. Very hot.

Shiitake mushrooms: Cultivated, full-flavored, dark brown "wild" mushrooms with broad caps ranging from 3 to 10 inches in diameter. Widely available both fresh and dried.

Star anise: A dried, star-shaped pod filled with tiny, pungent seeds. The licorice-flavored spice is used mainly in Asian cooking and is most easily found in Asian markets.

Tamarind: Fruit of the tamarind tree, often used in Indian, African, and Asian cooking to impart a sweet-sour flavor. Sold as a paste, syrup, pulp, powder, or dried bricks.

CONVERSION CHART

WEIGHTS AND MEASURES

1 teaspoon = 5 milliliters
1 tablespoon = 3 teaspoons = 15 milliliters
1/8 cup = 2 tablespoons = 1 fluid ounce = 30 milliliters
1/4 cup = 4 tablespoons = 2 fluid ounces = 59 milliliters
1/2 cup = 8 tablespoons = 4 fluid ounces = 118 milliliters
1 cup = 16 tablespoons = 8 fluid ounces = 237 milliliters
1 pint = 2 cups = 16 fluid ounces = 473 milliliters
1 quart = 4 cups = 32 fluid ounces = 946 milliliters (.946 liter)
1 gallon = 4 quarts = 16 cups = 128 fluid ounces = 3.78 liters

1 ounce = 28 grams
1/4 pound = 4 ounces = 114 grams
1 pound = 16 ounces = 454 grams
2.2 pounds = 1,000 grams = 1 kilogram

Index

Appaloosa, Butterscotch, and Chestnut Bean Salad, 37
Apricots Baked with Kirsch and Vanilla, 80
Asparagus and Morel Bruschetta, 23
Asparagus Salad with Littleneck Clams and Thyme, 21
Baba Ghanoosh, 60
Baked Peaches with Warm Blueberry-Thyme Sauce, 79
Banana-Guava Ketchup, 46
Banana-Pineapple Shake, 79
Bartolotta, Paul, 8, 70
Batali, Mario, 8, 23, 56, 69
Bean, Zucchini, and Pepper Salad, 53
Beans, appaloosa, butterscotch, and chestnut salad, 37
Beans, cooking, 15
Bergougnoux, Jean-Michel, 8, 51
Big Easy Seafood-Okra Gumbo, 68
Black Bean Broth, 56
Blackberry-Rhubarb Phyllo Tart, 84
Boniato Purée, 56
Boulud, Daniel, 8, 33, 67, 79
Bow Tie Pasta with Musselsand Zucchini, 70
Braised Beef with Bean, Zucchini, and Pepper Salad, 51
Braised Wild Mushrooms with Roasted Garlic Toasts, 21
Brody, Jane, 7, 8, 26, 37, 86
Broiled Pompano with Pickles and Vegetables, 67
Brown, Ed, 9, 63, 64
Caramelized Onion Pizza, 25
Carrot-Raisin Cake, 86
Cheese, blue with grilled peaches, 77
Chickpea spread, 26
Chilled Curried Tomato Soup with Cilantro Cream, 29
Chilled Summer Vegetable Soup with Spanish Vinegar and Quinoa Salad, 31
Cilantro Cream, 29
Clark, Patrick, 9, 40, 60
Cool Lamb Salad with Flageolet, Cumin, and Roasted Peppers, 56
Couscous and Sautéed Savoy Cabbage, 40
Crostini, whole wheat, 24
Cumin-Scented Yogurt, 57
De Gustibus, 6, 7
Dried Fig and Apricot Tart, 85

Eggplant and Crab Garbure with Cumin and Tomato Confit, 33
Emeril's Creole Seasoning, 69
Fish,
    pompano, broiled, with pickles and vegetables, 67
    salmon, roasted with Moroccan barbecue sauce, 60
    sole with tomato fondue and saffron pasta, 66
    striped bass with mango-black bean salsa, chayote squash and mango sauce, 63
    swordfish, grilled, and fennel with charred tomatoes and oil-roasted garlic, 64
    swordfish, spice-rubbed with mango-lime salsa, 61
Fruits,
    apricots baked with kirsch and vanilla, 80
    banana-guava ketchup, 46
    banana-pineapple shake, 79
    blackberry-rhubarb phyllo tart, 84
    blueberry-thyme sauce with baked peaches, 79
    citrus, zesting, 12
    cranberry, dried and port sauce, 49
    fig and apricot tart, 85
    mango-black bean salsa, 64
    mango-lime salsa, 61
    peaches, baked, with warm blueberry-thyme sauce, 79
    peaches, grilled, with blue cheese and sweet balsamic vinegar glaze, 77
    pears, roasted caramelized, 83
    pineapple ketchup, 54
    plum and ginger kuchen, 82
    pumpkin crème brûlée, 87
    raisin-carrot cake, 86
Fusilli with Twenty-Minute Tomato Sauce, Hot Chiles, and Arugula, 69
Gingered Green Bean Salad, 37
Grains,
    couscous and sautéed savoy cabbage, 40
    polenta, roasted, 20
    wild rice-orzo pilaf, 39
Grilled Honey-Basil Chicken, 45
Grilled Peaches with Blue Cheese and Sweet Balsamic Vinegar Glaze, 77

Grilled Swordfish and Fennel with Charred Tomatoes, Oil-Roasted Garlic, and Balsamic Vinegar, 64

Guerard, Michel, 7

Hamersley, Gordon, 9, 21

Herb-Marinated Chicken, Shiitake Mushrooms, and Roasted Potatoes Vinaigrette on Salad Greens, 48

Hook, Ron, 9, 37, 45, 87

Intercontinental Chickpea Spread, 26

Jamaican Jerk Chicken with Banana-Guava Ketchup, 46

Jamieson, Patricia, 7, 9, 25, 39, 49, 72, 84

Lagasse, Emeril, 10, 68

London Broil with Lime-Marinated Red Onions and Pineapple Ketchup, 53

Lukins, Sheila, 10, 30

Mango Sauce, 64

Mango-Black Bean Salsa, 64

Mango-Lime Salsa, 61

Marinated Flageolets, 57

Meat,
  beef, braised with bean, zucchini, and pepper salad, 51
  lamb salad with flageolet, cumin, and roasted peppers, 56
  lamb, leg of, with baba ghanoosh, 59
  london broil with marinated red onions and pineapple ketchup, 53
  pork over boniato purée with black bean broth, 55

Mercatelli, Valentino, 8

Militello, Mark, 10, 31

Oil-Roasted Garlic, 65

Orecchiette with Zucchini and Yellow Squash, 73

Parsley Salad with Bulgur, Mint, and Tomatoes, 38

Pasta,
  bow tie, with mussels and zucchini, 70
  cooking, 13
  fusilli with twenty-minute tomato sauce, hot chiles, and arugula, 69
  orecchiette with zucchini and yellow squash, 73
  orzo-wild rice pilaf, 39
  saffron and sole with tomato fondue, 66
  ziti with lentils and kale, 72

Patria Pork over Boniato Purée with Black Bean Broth, 55

Peel, Mark, 11, 40, 41, 59

Perrier, Georges, 10, 66

Pineapple Ketchup, 54

Pizza, caramelized onion, 25

Plum and Ginger Kuchen, 82

Potato Shoes, 40

Poultry,
  chicken, grilled honey-basil, 45
  chicken, herb-marinated, shiitake mushrooms, and roasted potatoes, 48
  chicken, Jamaican jerk with banana-guava ketchup, 46
  turkey breast, roasted with port and dried cranberry sauce, 49

Pumpkin Crème Brûlée, 87

Quick-Rising Pizza Dough, 25

Quinoa Salad, 32

Restaurants,
  Café Luxembourg, 9
  Campanile, 11
  East Coast Bar and Grill, 11
  Emeril's, 10
  Hamersley's Bistro, 9
  Jake and Earl's, 11
  L'Absinthe, 8
  La Brea Bakery, 11
  Le Bec Fin, 10
  Le Cirque, 8
  Le Cygne, 8
  Le Panetière, 10
  Le Régence, 8
  Lutèce, 8
  Mark's Los Olas, 10
  Mark's Place, 10
  Metro, 9
  Nola, 10
  Odeon, 9
  Pó, 8
  Restaurant Daniel, 8
  San Domenico Ristorante, 8
  SeaGrill, 9
  Spiaggia, 8
  Tavern on the Green, 9
  The Blue Room, 11
  Tropica, 9
  Yuca Restaurant, 10
  Patria, 10

Roasted Caramelized Pears, 83

Roasted Onions with Mustard Vinaigrette, 41

Roasted Peppers, 12, 57

Roasted Polenta, 20
Roasted Salmon with Moroccan Barbecue Sauce, 60
Roasted Sweet Potatoes, 39
**Roasted Turkey Breast with Port and Dried Cranberry
    Sauce**, 49
Roasting, vegetables, 12
Rodriguez, Douglas, 10, 27, 55
Salads,
    appaloosa, butterscotch, and chestnut bean, 37
    bean, zucchini, and pepper salad with braised beef, 51
    gingered green bean, 37
    lamb with flageolet, cumin, and roasted peppers, 56
    parsley with bulgur, mint, and tomatoes, 38
    quinoa, 32
Salsas,
    mango-black bean, 64
    mango-lime, 61
Sauce Hachée, 51
Sauces,
    Moroccan barbecue, 60
    port and dried cranberry, 49
    tomato with hot chiles, 69
    warm blueberry-thyme, 79
Schlesinger, Chris, 11, 38, 46, 53, 61, 77
Schneider, Sally, 7, 11, 19, 79, 80, 83
Seafood,
    clams and asparagus salad, 21
    crab and eggplant garbure with cumin and tomato confit,
        33
    mussels with bow tie pasta and zucchini, 70
    —-okra gumbo, 68
Shrimp Ceviche, 27
Silverton, Nancy, 11, 40, 41, 59
Simmons, Marie, 7, 11, 24, 29, 48, 73, 82, 85
Smothered Escarole on Whole Wheat Crostini, 24
Sole with Tomato Fondue and Saffron Pasta, 66
Soups,
    chilled curried tomato with cilantro cream, 29
    chilled summer vegetable with Spanish vinegar and
        quinoa salad, 31
    eggplant and crab garbure with cumin and tomato confit,
        33
    sweet pepper and yellow pepper, 30
Spice-Rubbed Swordfish with Mango-Lime Salsa, 61

Stocks,
    chicken, 14
    fish, 14
**Striped Bass with Mango-Black Bean Salsa, Chayote
    Squash and Mango Sauce**, 63
Sweet Pepper and Yellow Pepper Soup, 30
The Best Leg of Lamb with Baba Ghanoosh, 59
Tomato Confit, 33
Tomato Fondue, 66
Vegetables,
    arugula, hot chiles, and tomato sauce with fusilli, 69
    asparagus and morel bruschetta, 23
    asparagus salad with clams and thyme, 21
    bean, zucchini, and pepper salad with braised beef, 51
    blanching, 12
    boniato purée, with pork and black bean broth, 55
    cabbage, savoy sautéed and couscous, 40
    carrot-raisin cake, 86
    chayote squash, with striped bass, mango-black bean
        salsa, and mango sauce, 63
    chiles, preparing, 13
    chiles, roasting, 12
    chilled summer soup, 31
    cutting, 12
    eggplant and crab garbure with cumin and tomato confit,
        33
    escarole on whole wheat crostini, 24
    fennel with charred tomatoes and oil-roasted garlic with
        swordfish, 64
    garlic, oil-roasted, 65
    garlic, roasted, 15
    garlic, roasted toasts, 21
    green bean, gingered salad, 37
    kale with ziti and lentils, 72
    mushrooms, morel and asparagus bruschetta, 23
    mushrooms, shiitake, with herb-marinated chicken, 48
    mushrooms, wild braised with roasted garlic toasts, 21
    mushrooms, wild ragout with roasted polenta, 19
    okra-seafood gumbo, 68
    onion, caramelized pizza, 25
    onions, red marinated with london broil and pineapple
        ketchup, 53
    onions, roasted with mustard vinaigrette, 41
    pepper, sweet and yellow soup, 30
    peppers, roasted, flageolet, cumin and lamb salad, 56

Vegetables *(continued)*
  peppers, roasting, 12
  potato shoes, 40
  roasting, 12
  sweet potatoes, roasted, 39
  tomato confit, 33
  tomato fondue, 66
  tomato soup with cilantro cream, 29
  tomatoes, charred, with fennel, oil-roasted garlic and
    swordfish, 64
  tomatoes, parsley, bulgur, and mint salad, 38

Vegetables *(continued)*
  vegetables with pompano and pickles, 67
  zucchini and yellow squash with orecchiette, 73
  zucchini with mussels and bow tie pasta, 70
Vinaigrette, mustard, 41
Warm Blueberry-Thyme Sauce, 80
Wild Mushroom Ragout with Roasted Polenta, 19
Wild Rice-Orzo Pilaf, 39
Zesting, fruits, 12
Ziti with Lentils and Kale, 72